THE END

The Unique Voice of Adventists About the Return of Jesus

by
Herbert E. Douglass

TEACH Services, Inc.
Brushton, New York

**PRINTED IN
THE UNITED STATES OF AMERICA**

World rights reserved. This book or any portion thereof may not be copied or reproduced in any form or manner whatever, except as provided by law, without the written permission of the publisher, except by a reviewer who may quote brief passages in a review. The author assumes full responsibility for the accuracy of all facts and quotations as cited in this book.

Facsimile Reproduction

As this book played a formative role in the development of Christian thought and the publisher feels that this book, with its candor and depth, still holds significance for the church today. Therefore the publisher has chosen to reproduce this historical classic from an original copy. Frequent variations in the quality of the print are unavoidable due to the condition of the original. Thus the print may look darker or lighter or appear to be missing detail, more in some places than in others.

2010 11 12 13 14 · 5 4 3 2 1

Copyright © 2001 TEACH Services, Inc.
ISBN-13: 978-1-57258-217-0
Library of Congress Control Number: 2001093759

Published by

TEACH Services, Inc.
www.TEACHServices.com

To
my mother and father,
Mildred and Herbert Douglass, Sr.,
who recognized the intrinsic worth of the
Adventist message when the author was a
young teenager and provided unrelenting
encouragement for his schooling and ministry
as the years rolled on.

May the Lord be praised for parents who forgo personal benefits
so that their children may catch swiftly passing
opportunities.

Contents

Introduction	9
Growing Adventist Dilemmas	13
Modern Interest in the End of the World	21
Conflicting Doctrines of the Second Advent	32
The Principle of Conditional Prophecy	58
The Harvest Principle	65
They Refused "To Know"	83
What Jesus Waits For	92
Between Now and Then	118
God's People Vindicate His Government	132
Adventism's Highest Priority	141
APPENDIX A Ellen G. White Statements Regarding a Delayed Advent	161
APPENDIX B Statements of Imminent Advent Through the Centuries	168
APPENDIX C A Plausible Scenario	176
APPENDIX D Annual Council Appeals, 1973 and 1974	178
Indexes	190

All Bible quotations are from the Revised Standard Version unless otherwise indicated.

Introduction

This volume is not a doctrinal study of the second advent; no attempt is here made to develop a biblical exposition of the Seventh-day Adventist doctrine of the literal return of Jesus. Other books, such as *Seventh-day Adventist Encyclopedia* (Washington: Review and Herald Publishing Association, 1976), pp. 1306-1309; Robert H. Pierson, *Good-bye, Planet Earth* (Mountain View, California: Pacific Press Publishing Association, 1976); M. L. Andreasen, *Faith of Jesus* (Washington: Review and Herald Publishing Association, 1949), pp. 219-294; H. M. S. Richards, Sr., *How Will Jesus Come?* (Glendale, California: The Voice of Prophecy, 1960); and Fernando Chaij, *The Impending Drama* (Nashville: Southern Publishing Association, 1979), reflect the general Adventist position.

The author presumes that the reader knows this position that looks forward to a literal, visible return of Jesus Himself—an event that will bring to a close the flow of human history (as we know it).

Nor does this volume attempt to outline *how* a person becomes a Christian or *how* Christian character is developed and sins overcome. Other books have focused on these subjects. Some are Ellen G. White, *Steps to Christ* (Mountain View, California: Pacific Press Publishing Association); George E. Vandeman, *Sail Your Own Seas* (Mountain View, California: Pacific Press Publishing Association, 1975); Ted Torkelson, *One Heart, One Vote* (Mountain View, California: Pacific Press Publishing Association, 1975); and Thomas A. Davis, *How to Be a Victorious Christian* (Washington: Review and Herald Publishing Association, 1975).

The author again assumes that the reader knows the basic Adventist position regarding how men and women are saved: In open and tragic conflict with his origin and created purpose, Everyman senses, even though dimly, his loss and his helplessness. In varying degrees he realizes his predicament, that somehow he has lost his spiritual home. But no matter what he thinks or does, Everyman cannot erase his worst fears regarding the future, or solve the perennial problems of human existence, such as crime and war, or ease his guilt for personal irresponsibilities.

Everyman needs help from outside the human circle—and that help comes from the Creator God against whom he has rebelled. Adventists believe that in Jesus Christ, God has entered the human drama. Through His life and death Jesus became Everyman's Substitute. Upon Him who knew no sin rested the consequences and penalty of Everyman's sins. Without this incredible gift to the human race, focused in that awful experience called Calvary, reconciliation with God would have been impossible and thus no pardon, no peace in forgiveness, no reinstatement as reclaimed children to a heavenly Father, no power over sins that destroy Everyman's best intentions, no hope for a better day and a future without sin and its consequences—if Jesus had not come to earth as Everyman's Surety. In Him is our peace and the basis of Everyman's complete atonement with God.

In this present volume, however, the author focuses on one particular aspect of the second advent and on how all Christians should relate to the current worldwide emphasis on the end of the world. Along with others, he is aware of the growing dilemmas within the Christian church in general and within the Seventh-day Adventist Church specifically, during (what some have called) the time of the delayed advent. Obviously, many questions now arise that never would have been conceived if Jesus had come a century ago. That is, *if* He should have come a century ago!

Nevertheless, how do Adventists in particular relate to a lengthening period, at the beginning of which they proclaimed the imminent return of Jesus?

Has the Adventist Church generally focused on those conditions which determine how soon Jesus may return? Can the church afford to contribute to the emotional fatigue generated whenever the latest world crisis or happening is repeatedly designated as the "sign" that the end of the world is at hand? Are there any lessons to learn from Aesop's little story about the shepherd boy and the wolf?

The reader will examine the causes of the current emphasis on the end of the world; they are not all religious, nor all biological and physical. The various conflicting voices within Christianity describing how and when the end will come will be reviewed.

Certain basic biblical principles that aid in interpreting the biblical message, such as conditional prophecy and the harvest principle, will be discussed. The author recognizes that the harvest principle in the Bible is more implicit than explicit but feels, with others, that it helps to focus the Bible's fundamental intent regarding the second advent.

Particular attention will be directed to our Lord's analogy comparing Noah's experience before the Flood and that of the last generation living when probationary time closes.

Primary attention will be given to a positive picture of what Jesus did say about the kind of people who will be ready for His return—and what they will be doing to hasten that day.

A very condensed outline of those general events yet to transpire between the present and the return of Jesus will be studied.

Accepting the biblical teaching that Christians are more than spectators in the plan of salvation—that indeed they are active participants, not only in the saving of their own souls but in the vindicating of God's method of dealing with sin—a special chapter is devoted to examining how God's faithful vindicate His name and government.

Summarizing the focus of the book, the last chapter will concentrate on practical questions that serious Seventh-day Adventists are now discussing the world over. The burden of responsibility deepens the humility of sober Adventists. Who is sufficient for these things?

The Lord is gracious to us all—far more than anyone deserves. His mysterious hand of providence etches love, compassion, and design in the experience of the grateful. Above all, He is not something to talk about, but Somebody to know. He personally commits Himself to be heard within the inner precincts of the soul whenever we trace His thoughts in Holy Scripture; He will be His own witness that His words are true and everlasting.

The author acknowledges those innumerable scholars who have added to the clarification of truth through the years; to his teachers, such as Lewis Hartin at Atlantic Union College, the galaxy at the Seventh-day Adventist Theological Seminary during the early 1950s; to such luminous friends as Harland Hogue and Durwood Foster at the Pacific School of Religion, Berkeley, California; to his incredibly patient and adored children, Janelle, Herbert III, Reatha, and Vivienne Sue—all of whom have filled that rimless reservoir of cheer, goodwill, and knowledge from which the author draws courage and insight.

But to that person of charm and industry, without whom the manuscript would never have been written, typed, and finished during a rather intimidating schedule, I owe my special and enduring thanks—to Norma.

Growing Adventist Dilemmas

For years now, Seventh-day Adventists have been celebrating centennials. The *Adventist Review,* our church paper, published its centennial issue in 1950 and its 125th Anniversary issue in 1975; *The Youth's Instructor* (now, *Insight*), in 1952. We saluted Buck's Bridge, New York, after 100 years of church schools in 1953; the founding of our first local conference (Michigan, 1861) in 1961; and in 1974 the establishment of Andrews University plus the momentous occasion of sending our first foreign missionary. The costumes, the impersonations, the nostalgia, stopwatch programming —all done with style and propriety. Every passing year adds an increasing number of schools, hospitals, churches, and conferences celebrating their first 100 years.

How should Seventh-day Adventists celebrate centennials? Are we supposed to be happy or sad? In view of our mission, are they a sign of success, or something much less plausible? A celebration, or a time for sober reflection?

From 1844 to the present is a long time. Were the Adventists of a century ago premature in announcing that Jesus was to return in their day, that His coming was near, even at the doors? Were they zealous but theologically incorrect? Fourteen decades is a long time to preach that Christ's coming is imminent, that He is at the door! How near is "near" when men and women grow old and die with the Adventist hope on their lips—a lifetime of believing that Jesus' coming "is near."

In a recent General Conference committee, a longtime friend submitted his letter of resignation. In a farewell speech he reflected, "Here is a letter which I never thought I would ever have to write. When I began my ministry fifty years ago, I surely thought the Lord would have come before now."

THE END: THE UNIQUE VOICE OF ADVENTISTS

There was hardly a dry eye. The silence said it all.

After our family became Seventh-day Adventists and I left home for Atlantic Union College in 1943, the literature evangelists who nourished us in our growing faith—mature, intelligent, committed men—pleaded with me to join them in the literature ministry. I remember their words well: "Herb, there is not enough time left to finish college. Join us in bringing the gospel directly to the people. The Lord will be here before you finish college."

What happened? Should early Adventists be given high grades for zeal but an F for poor research? No, our pioneers were not incorrect. The generation that preached the judgment hour message beginning in 1844 could have been and should have been the last, as we are often reminded.[1]

ONLY ADVENTISTS KNOW WHY

But, though correct in theology, Seventh-day Adventists have not been faithful to their theology.[2] Although we believe that Jesus has delayed His coming, we seem not to be eager to discover why. To believe that Jesus is in a holding pattern is perhaps one of the greatest concepts that anyone on earth can encounter; the awesome truth is that only Seventh-day Adventists are able to tell the world why!

Some feel that Adventists are talking less about the advent in the last quarter of the twentieth century than they ever did. Some feel that the rearranging of priorities, the reordering of life patterns and institutional activities that would help to hasten the advent are discussed even less.

If this is so, why the reluctance? Would it be partly because of the suffocating demands and pleasures of this world, where even the good is the enemy of the best? Would it be partly due to the slackening of diligent Bible study that once distinguished Seventh-day Adventists?

But more than correct information is needed. In writing this book I am concerned about correct thinking, but much more. The five foolish bridesmaids (Matthew 25) had no less information about the second advent than the five wise. In fact, for all practical purposes, they were "good" Seventh-day Adventists. They knew the theory of truth, could answer well in their Sabbath School class or on their academy or college Bible examinations, and could even convince their neighbors that the seventh-day was the Sabbath and that Jesus was soon returning. But the foolish bridesmaids did not let their thinking alter their basic life-style; they did not permit the Holy Spirit to do His work of transforming their lives so that they reflected the character of Jesus.[3] They had no light—just doctrinal information!

And more than sincerity is needed. Sincerely believing what he knew about God did not save the slothful servant, who in the end heard, "Take the talent from him." Matthew 25:28. Devoted to self-serving, contributing to the church's need or his neighbor's only when it is convenient, the slothful servant eventually reaches that horrible place where he really has nothing left to give.

Those represented by the sincere servant who played it cool are not gross sinners. Although they neglected the claims of God on their lives, thinking perhaps that works don't figure in the gospel equation as long as they claim God's redemptive justification, they did "not feel that in this there is any wrong. They know that the blasphemer, the murderer, the adulterer deserves punishment; but as for them, they enjoy the services of religion. They love to hear the gospel preached, and therefore they think themselves Christians."[4]

Even sincere men and women will hear the dreadful decree, "Take the talent from" them.

SINCERELY BUSY PEOPLE ARE SURPRISED

But not only the sincerely passive will be surprised. Jesus indicated that many very busy people—sincerely busy people—will be surprised. "Not every one who says to me, 'Lord, Lord,' shall enter the kingdom of heaven, but he who does the will of my Father who is in heaven. On that day many will say to me, 'Lord, Lord, did we not prophesy in your name, and cast out demons in your name, and do many mighty works in your name?' And then will I declare to them, 'I never knew you; depart from me, you evildoers.'" Matthew 7:21-23.

THE END: THE UNIQUE VOICE OF ADVENTISTS

Charlie Brown can drag his bat and plead for understanding, day after day, as he loses one ball game after another. That one day when he lost 174 - 0 was especially painful. In utter frustration, he cries out, "How can we lose when we are so sincere?"

Many more important things than ball games are lost by sincere people. School promotions, marriages, careers, long-standing friendships—all have been lost by sincere people. So easy to settle into a respectable, church-member mediocrity—and be sincere.

So we are concerned in this book with something more than correct information, although we cannot go far without it. We are concerned with something more than sincerity, although no Christian can properly breathe without it. We are concerned with whatever Jesus is waiting for that will hasten His return. We will examine why He waits for credible witnesses, believable witnesses, who can so represent Him that to reject their witness is the same as to reject Him. We will note that He will not withdraw His protective shield from earth's billions, permitting agencies of evil to unleash their awful deviltry, unless every person has been given a fair, compelling opportunity to accept His way of life. He waits for a people about whom He can say, "Here they are, take a good look at them. Here are 'those who keep the commandments of God and the faith of Jesus.' " See Revelation 14:12.

MORE THAN A THEOLOGICAL DILEMMA

In addition to their strange reluctance to face their theological dilemma, Seventh-day Adventists cannot ignore other dilemmas such as the temptation to substitute many good and laudable works for their greatest assignment. Or, relaxing with almost smug "I told you so's" to the world that has come around to their thinking. Or, experiencing a strange bafflement while watching other groups take their lines and shout them louder. In the last quarter of the twentieth century some have observed a tendency to seek approval while muting distinctives, to bask in kind words, awards, plaques, and command performances before presidents and

GROWING ADVENTIST DILEMMAS

kings. Adventists are no longer lonely. The issues that Adventists almost single-handedly kept before the world for more than a century have become front-page issues of inescapable importance for almost everybody—from the man on the street to the specialists who wrestle with their implications. Such subjects as the future of life on this planet, the quality of life, the dignity and freedom of individuals, and personal meaning to man's existence—all are suddenly chief concerns of modern men and women, especially in the last decade. Books discussing these traditional Adventist topics are phenomenal best-sellers.

Without question, young and old are discussing the future of this planet as never before.[5] Alvin Toffler's book on *Future Shock*[6] has been an astounding best-seller; its title alone has coined a phrase now commonplace.

But talk about the future is an Adventist trademark. For many decades the Adventist voice was a lonely, disturbing element in a world where most men and women saw nothing but golden gleams of a future free from war, hunger, poverty, and greed. For years Adventists were known as the "calamity howlers." Not so, today. Yet, fundamental differences remain between Adventist thinking about the future and whatever else is being said by those who outshout our own dire predictions—and these radical differences will be discussed in later chapters.

For a century Adventists have been appealing to the world to listen to the gospel of good health. We have implored our neighbors to stop smoking and drinking, to take physical exercise seriously, to reduce animal product consumption—even to reduce intake of salt, sugar, oils, and fats. We surely were in the vanguard of those mighty forces of today that teach the close relationship between the physical, the mental, the emotional, the moral, and the spiritual. But Adventists emphasize the stewardship of the body for different reasons than most others who share our concerns. This, too, we will discuss in later chapters.

In recent decades a phenomenal concern for human rights and individual freedom has arisen around the world. Adventists are still among the leaders who aggressively teach that

THE END: THE UNIQUE VOICE OF ADVENTISTS

religious freedom is an inalienable right under God, regardless of where a person lives. Yet, the Adventist emphasis has dimensions that few others share. We understand why emphasis on human rights may degenerate into waves of sentimentalism, then anarchy, and finally the permissiveness of ultimate subjectivism because of an inadequate understanding of sin. But Adventists are also aware of the inevitable reaction by the majority to the freedoms of minorities in times of national calamity, a frightening prospect so often experienced through the centuries; they know that the world is headed for centralized government and political repression such as has never before been seen on this planet.

Adventists can tell the truth about personal meaning, especially as it relates to true self-development. They know the close relationship between obedience to the laws of God and the truly unshackled, free, man or woman. They know that there is no character development or ultimate salvation in merely remembering Bible texts and agreeing to denominational doctrine; the serious Adventist knows that unless the voice of Jesus is personally heard and obeyed when the Bible is studied, religion soon becomes an unhappy, meaningless burden or bore.

My point is this: we may bask in our contributions and revel in accolades; but if the Adventist dimension is muted—if the purpose of our Adventist advantage in these insights regarding the future, the quality of life, the dignity of man, and the route to personal fulfillment is blunted or ignored or diluted—the mission of the Seventh-day Adventist Church is on a course of self-destruction.

THE ADVENTIST ADVANTAGE

This book is about dilemmas resting on those who possess the Adventist advantage—and thus the Adventist responsibility. Make no mistake about it. There is not the slightest reason to falter at this point: Adventists have the advantage. They can speak out convincingly anywhere—in the humble cottage or the sophisticated university seminar, or over any backyard fence. Wherever men and women search for truth about the future, the quality of life, human rights, and mean-

GROWING ADVENTIST DILEMMAS

ing to personal existence, Seventh-day Adventists need have no uneasy feeling that they may be riding only a temporary wave or a sentimental fad.

The Adventist mission is not merely to make correct thinkers out of seventh-day Sabbath keepers nor to make them the healthiest men and women in the neighborhood—breaking all records in longevity—nor to say what others are saying, only louder.

What the world considers important today have been Adventist subjects for more than a century; the validity of their message has never been more vindicated. But the Adventist advantage and uniqueness lies not in any particular part of its message but in its integrated wholeness—and thus its purpose. The Adventist advantage has been given to the Seventh-day Adventist Church for one primary, central purpose with a double emphasis: to awaken a world to its impending judgment and to prepare a people to meet their Lord.

Unusual as it sounds, the University Christian Movement, with offices at the Interchurch Center, New York City, voted itself out of existence in 1968. On their door was posted this sign: "Gone out of business—didn't know what our business was."

How many churches today could post that statement, close down operations, and never be missed? How many churches are going through the motions, bearing the name of a great leader or tradition, but nourished not by its historic purpose? How many churches are either ignoring their dilemmas or rejecting their historical roots which once gave them a reason for existing?

The Seventh-day Adventist Church is not a faded leaf, nor a community of nice people groping for answers; they are a people with a special message for a special time. Not to "know what our business is" not only invites personal distress and aimlessness, but postpones the day until some generation of Seventh-day Adventists does take God and its denominational roots seriously. The Adventist mission is to remove the conditions that keep Jesus waiting, to alert men and women who seek truth and righteousness that God will

THE END: THE UNIQUE VOICE OF ADVENTISTS

be more than sufficient for their individual problems and will save them forever if they will only let Him be their Saviour from sin.

Regarding the end of the world and the return of Jesus, God has no contingency plans but to be true to Himself and to His way of dealing with sin as He has since the beginning of the great controversy. To Seventh-day Adventists has been given the assignment of making this theology of the great controversy known in simple terms. They are called to proclaim a message, not to create it.

Although the following pages may seem to focus on one aspect of the Adventist advantage and its accompanying dilemma—the knowledge of what God has on His mind regarding how this world will end, and the Adventist response—we will try to remind ourselves, the author and reader together, that Christians follow Christ; that living the truth is more important than knowing the truth; that God is more than able to take a people today through Red Seas, parched wildernesses, and swollen Jordans.

References

1. In chapter five we shall review the evidence that indicates Jesus should have returned in the nineteenth century. See Appendix A for Ellen White statements regarding the advent delay.
2. See Appendix D for the Annual Council Appeals of 1973 and 1974 wherein messages went out to Adventist churches the world over, messages that the Adventist Church had not heard for years.
3. Ellen G. White, *Christ's Object Lessons* (Washington, D.C.: Review and Herald Publishing Association, 1900), p. 384.
4. *Ibid.*, p. 365.
5. More than 130 separate futurist organizations, associations, or groups are listed in the Appendix of Hiley H. Ward, *Religion 2101 A.D.* (Garden City, N.Y.: Doubleday and Company, Inc., 1975).
6. Alvin Toffler, *Future Shock* (New York: Bantam Books, 1970).

Modern Interest in the End of the World

Who would have believed twenty-five years ago, or even ten years ago, that American highways in the 1970s would be rampant with car bumpers announcing, "Guess Who's Coming Again," "Honk, If You Love Jesus," "In Case of Rapture, This Vehicle Self-Destructs," or "In Case of Rapture, Grab the Wheel"?

Who would have believed that books on the last-day prophecies would become best-sellers, such as Hal Lindsey's *The Late Great Planet Earth,*[1] which sold more than ten million copies in only a few years?[2] Or that a warmed-over 1924 chestnut, *The Millennium Bible*, by William E. Biederwolf, would sell more than fifty thousand copies in the first five months after it was resurrected under the new title, *The Second Coming Bible*?[3]

In fact, even a corporation was founded in 1973, Second Coming, Inc., by Salem Kirban, a longtime familiar name to students of Bible prophecy. His books include *Your Last Goodbye* and *666*, both best-sellers in recent years.

But one would not have to be a great reader to catch the message. Radio and television have flooded cars and homes with the unashamed candor of young and old as they witness to a new life in Jesus and their belief in His soon return. Football heroes, entertainment stars, successful businessmen—the chorus is swelling: "Jesus is coming soon."

But who would have dreamed of believing a few years ago that a sophisticated church of 2000 members in North Hollywood, California, situated on one of the city's busiest corners, would become so serious about the imminent return of Jesus that it would take legal steps to provide for continued church leadership when its officers are suddenly taken to heaven in what they call "the secret rapture"!

In a move that must be given first prize for farsighted

THE END: THE UNIQUE VOICE OF ADVENTISTS

action, the congregation voted to have those church members who didn't make it in the first go-around to get together at 11:00 a.m., the Sunday after Christ's return, so that a temporary chairman could be named and a new church council formed. The idea is that the remaining members—those who weren't first-class—would organize themselves so that the $1.5 million property could keep going, helping to fight the onslaught of the antichrist who would trouble the earth for the intervening seven years before Jesus, with a crashing finale, returned in judgment.

But that is not all. These church members, along with the other church groups, are making further legal preparation to outwit the devil and antichrist. Because it takes money to operate a church while the saints are in heaven with Jesus, church members are changing their wills and insurance policies to make the church their beneficiary in case of rapture. Mutual of New York already has indicated that when the millions of saints are caught up in the air it is willing to "make immediate payment of the policy proceeds without waiting the usual seven years as is the case of 'missing persons.' "[4]

However, if the insurance companies do not pay off for some reason, they are to delay payment until after the seventh year, when all raptured Christians are scheduled to return to earth with Christ. All their money and estates will then be waiting for them, forever beyond the grasp of the devil and greedy neighbors. In other words suggesting, that if you can't take it with you, make sure it is waiting for you when you get back!

The recital of second-coming phenomena could go on for a long time.[5]

WORLD ACCUSTOMED TO END-OF-WORLD TALK

Strange as it may seem, especially for Seventh-day Adventists, who have been the target of either disdain or ridicule for a century, we are now living in a world very accustomed to hearing about the second advent! The simple fact is that people today are talking about the end of the world and the return of Jesus to a degree not seen or heard

MODERN INTEREST IN THE END OF THE WORLD

since the second quarter of the nineteenth century.

However, what almost every church or religious magazine is proclaiming today regarding the return of Jesus is contrary to what Seventh-day Adventists understand to be the truth about the advent.

Furthermore, in this unprecedented surge of interest in the second advent, among the books selling in the hundreds of thousands, even millions, there is not one written by a Seventh-day Adventist. When this modern religious phenomenon is commented on in the secular press, many persons and churches are referred to as its responsible leaders and driving forces, but in no instance have we read of a reference to Seventh-day Adventists as one of these leading influences.

What does all this mean? Have Seventh-day Adventists become passé, having served their time, and now must more dynamic voices be heard? Why aren't Seventh-day Adventists in midstream, surrounded by millions who have suddenly discovered how correct Seventh-day Adventists have been all these years? Why hasn't the Lord come, if our pioneers were correct a century ago in proclaiming that His coming was near? Should not He have come before the turn of the twentieth century?

These questions and others must be answered straight on and soon by all Seventh-day Adventists, leadership and laity alike. Each member's sense of reality and personal mission is involved; the church's sense of purpose and destiny is inextricably involved in its answers.

This modest volume will not attempt to respond directly to these central and inescapable questions—except to focus on one facet of Adventist truth regarding the second advent. We will examine reasons for the delay in Christ's return, and trust that a renewed study will motivate us all to an accelerated completion of the church's task. Truth always carries with it its own urgency, and God knows how little urgency impels His church today.

Quietly, yet firmly, we note that such a focus would not occur to any other church on earth today; therein lies the background and urgency for a discussion of the uniqueness

THE END: THE UNIQUE VOICE OF ADVENTISTS

of Adventist theology regarding the second advent of Jesus Christ. The Seventh-day Adventist Church has an understanding about the advent that will unravel the complex non sequiturs and pending disillusionments built into almost every voice now proclaiming the imminent end of the world. With that understanding comes a heavy responsibility to Seventh-day Adventists—to lead honest seekers for truth everywhere into the restfulness and excitement of a coherent biblical picture of how this world will come to its end.

Before we proceed directly into an examination of various, conflicting teachings that the world is hearing these days regarding the end of the world, we should pause for a moment and ask, Why? How come this modern surge of interest in the end of the world and in the return of Jesus? The answer comes in at least four parts: (1) disillusionment with modern technology; (2) fear of an earth-destroying nuclear war; (3) the seeming, all-pervasive moral collapse; and (4) the reestablishment of the state of Israel.

For a large segment of Western civilization especially, technology itself has become man's self-inflicted wound and is hastening his day of doom. Disillusionment with modern technology—the fear of living on a planet with its built-in, self-destructing time bomb ticking away—is expressed in life-styles ranging from those who retreat to their "caves" to get away from it all, to those who climb on the nearest, ever faster, merry-go-round to get the most of sensual satisfaction out of life before it all stops. The rich and poor, the trained and unschooled, are often united in expressing their disillusionment over once-cherished hopes that science and technology would solve human problems.

Chief among the disillusioning factors are the crises involving the ecology-energy tension; the worldwide raw material depletion; and the population explosion. Each area, in itself, is monumental in global importance. When these are added together, those pessimistic about the future see only chaos. Yet, paradoxically, each crisis is a by-product of mankind's amazing leap in knowledge over the past fifty years.

The price we have paid for the quantum leap in industrial

MODERN INTEREST IN THE END OF THE WORLD

expansion, producing undreamed of comforts and conveniences of modern society, has been polluted air and waterways. The energy required to fuel this remarkable increase in the world's standard of living and the raw materials necessary to make it happen have been enormous, leading many to serious thought regarding how long such consumption can last. Some experts do not give the world another twenty-five years.[6] The consequence of improved medical procedures and medicines plus new light on nutrition and its effect on preventing illness is simply that fewer babies die in infancy and more people live longer than ever before. Because land does not increase and those occupying land do, many specialists in population control predict dire consequences in the foreseeable future for an overcrowded planet.

Recently the Club of Rome celebrated it tenth anniversary. Since its formation in April 1968, this group of thirty representative leaders from the worlds of technology, business, science, politics, and academia have seriously studied the factors, in their opinion, which are hastening world collapse. Beginning with their first publication, *The Limits to Growth*,[7] they have spoken out periodically against the modern fever of growth and proliferation of new products, stating unequivocally that unless drastic changes are made immediately, this planet will not survive.

Aurelio Peccei, the club's president on the occasion of its tenth anniversary, said that "the world situation has deteriorated on all fronts. There have of course been techno-scientific improvements, but they have been unsystematic, uncoordinated, and many of them have caused other problems of a political and social nature. So altogether man is more confused today, more worried and less secure, than ten years ago.... We issued a warning ten years ago, but looking back we feel it was so easy to do something then, and so difficult now. However, doing something now is much more necessary. We think that mankind has perhaps only ten years or less to choose a course different from the present one, which is bound to end in disaster."[8]

Whether these modern fears generated by the fallout from fantastic technological advances are warranted is the subject

THE END: THE UNIQUE VOICE OF ADVENTISTS

of serious debate. But the fact remains that a very large group of intelligent people believe that this planet is on collision course with either built-in man-made time bombs or global catastrophes from nature gone wild or from forces extraterrestrial. A page in *Time* (March 5, 1979) was devoted to "The Deluge of Disastermania," describing Armageddon as a "growth industry."

But there are the optimists[9] who believe that rational, innovative men and women will always "come up" with solutions to potentially devastating problems (such as the elevator when the cities mushroomed, and the computer when record keeping was drowning the business world in paper).

Yet, many of these technological optimists face other problems that indicate civilization is living in its last days. They view the years since the founding of the United Nations in 1948 to have been all downhill. Born amidst prayerful hopes that the nations had at last found a mechanism whereby war would be prevented, the United Nations Organization has been described as this world's last chance.

FEAR OF NUCLEAR DISASTER

Today probably few organizations have less credibility than the United Nations, especially when considering its effectiveness to restrain border wars, never mind a global nuclear war. Its inability in the last thirty years to halt aggressions, large or small, has evaporated the last hope of most men and women that World War III can be averted, especially when a world power troubled with economic insecurity chooses to unleash its nuclear arsenal in a preemptive "first strike."

Representing the voice of many world leaders is Senator Daniel P. Moynihan, former U.S. ambassador to the United Nations. In an address at the opening of the new Pace University law center January 27, 1979, he said that totalitarian governments have succeeded in destroying the role of the United Nations and the United States as the world's primary keepers of the peace.

He went on to say, "The totalitarians now have a working

MODERN INTEREST IN THE END OF THE WORLD

majority and the institution [United Nations] responds increasingly to totalitarian norms. . . . This would not have been the case when the United Nations was first formed."

Moynihan also said that the United States, as part of the United Nations, has failed to "respond to the violations of the charter" such as have occurred so frequently in the last thirty years.[10]

Commenting on the markedly renewed emphasis on biblical authority and personal spirituality among seminary students in 1979 compared to an earlier decade, "Doward McBain, president of the American Baptist Seminary of the West, pinpointed the most important reason: 'The dangerous world in which we live, in which great powers can vaporize most of civilization, has had its effect on theology. We're not permanent in this world.' "[11]

The *Bulletin of Atomic Scientists* has for years kept its prophesying clock before the world. The *Bulletin* is written by knowledgeable scientists and statesmen for thoughtful people everywhere. No one doubts the high credibility and personal credentials of those who feel constrained to get their message out: We live in a world only minutes from nuclear incineration.

Since 1947 the hour hand has been close to midnight, the minute hand advancing and retreating through the years depending upon the movement of international brinkmanship. Today the hands read, "Nine minutes to midnight." Almost every issue of the *Bulletin* contains an article that uses, or implies, the words "time is running out."

COLLAPSE OF MORAL INTEGRITY

Others see the end of the world as we know it in terms of the well-nigh universal collapse of moral integrity. To them the darkening shadows of moral twilight pose an even greater threat to civilization than ecological crises or potential nuclear annihilation. Representing this growing sector, Alexander Solzhenitsyn addressed the assembled faculty, graduates, and parents for the Harvard University commencement on June 8, 1978. His rejection of the Soviet system of solving human problems is well known, especially

THE END: THE UNIQUE VOICE OF ADVENTISTS

as chronicled in *The Gulag Archipelago*.[12]

But what he said at Harvard was an astounding analysis of what is wrong, not with Russia only, but with Western civilization as a whole, denouncing such evils as "civic cowardice, immoral legalism, a licentious press, capitulation in Asia, and godless humanism."[13]

The brilliant observer of his times said, "I have spent all my life under a Communist regime, and I will tell you that a society without any objective legal scale is a terrible one indeed. But a society with no other scale but the legal one is not quite worthy of man either. The letter of the law is too cold and formal to have a beneficial influence on society. Whenever the tissue of life is woven of legalistic relations, there is an atmosphere of moral mediocrity, paralyzing man's noblest impulses."[14]

In other words, when a society presses the letter of the law, it does little to impose self-restraint. Behavior is acceptable so long as some jury or judge considers such behavior within the limits of the law. Solzhenitsyn sees this "atmosphere of moral mediocrity" leading to the "abyss of human decadence."

What lies behind Solzhenitsyn's concern for our generation's slide into moral decadence? In carefully chosen words he placed much of the blame upon those who did not admit the existence of intrinsic evil in man. The result: the situation where "man's sense of responsibility to God grew dimmer and dimmer," as reflected in the tragic loss of the moral heritage of the Christian faith and the "great reserves of mercy and sacrifice" produced by it.[15]

THE STATE OF ISRAEL

For still others a more definite, more dramatic sign that the end is near exists—the 1948 establishment of the state of Israel. They base their excitement on certain biblical prophecies that they interpret to be fulfilled in the rise of a modern Jewish nation.

Dozens of books, if not hundreds, have been written in the last thirty years that echo Leon J. Wood's theme as unfolded in his book, *The Bible and Future Events*. Dr. Wood, pro-

MODERN INTEREST IN THE END OF THE WORLD

fessor of Old Testament Studies and dean of the Grand Rapids Baptist Bible Seminary, wrote this:

"The clearest sign of Christ's return is the modern state of Israel. The Scriptures teach that in the last days Jews will return to their land in large numbers, with a resultant reestablishment of their sovereign state."[16]

John Walvoord, president of Dallas Theological Seminary since 1952 and recognized authority for millions in the area of last-day events, stated his conviction:

"The emergence of Israel and the present struggle for international power in the Middle East may well be a note of warning that the end of the times of the Gentiles is only years away.[17]

"The present return of Israel to the land sets the stage for an important series of end-time events. The prophecies about the return will not be completely fulfilled until after the times of the Gentiles' race to an end at Armageddon.[18]

"Our present world is well prepared for the beginning of the prophetic drama that will lead to Armageddon. Since the stage is set for this dramatic climax of the age, it must mean that Christ's coming for His own is very near."[19]

Disillusionment with modern technology and its attendant problems of ecological imbalances, raw material depletions, and population explosion; disenchantment with the United Nations and all other human attempts to thwart nuclear disaster; frustration with the moral collapse in high places as well as throughout the social fabric generally; and the reestablishment of the modern state of Israel—all are phenomenal developments surfacing in the last thirty-five years.

Seventh-day Adventists are well aware of the worldwide coincidence and impact of these events. But Adventist belief that Jesus can return in our day is not primarily motivated by any of these reasons. For more than a century, they have preached that Jesus could have returned within the lifetime of any generation living since 1844—long before the world heard about population explosions, ecological imbalances, nuclear weapons, energy crises, Adolf Hitler, World War II, space flights, or the modern state of Israel.

Adventist reasons for expecting the return of Jesus any

time within the last century have rested on sound principles of interpreting the Bible and not on sensational headlines in the morning newspaper.

Nevertheless, many Seventh-day Adventists are in various degrees of wonderment and frustration as they watch and listen today. For so long they were considered the calamity howlers, the prophets of doom, lonely voices crying in the wilderness—while the rest of the world appeared to be moving into the golden tomorrow. But now, those that have been traditionally considered "apostate Protestants" are proclaiming, with far more public impact, the main theme of Adventism—"Jesus is coming soon." And they are using virtually the same texts that Adventists had been using! Worse yet, they come up with different conclusions!

The questions What's going on? Have Adventists missed a signal? are understandable. But the answers grow out of the fundamental observation that what most every other church or religious journal is proclaiming regarding the end of the world and the return of Jesus runs contrary to what Seventh-day Adventists understand to be the truth about the second advent.

Consequently, to understand better the present confusion among the many voices that proclaim the nearness of the advent, the reader should have at least a passing awareness of these various camps, both liberal and conservative. They should note their doctrinal positions and how they differ with Seventh-day Adventists. Otherwise, our claim to uniqueness would appear meaningless. In the next chapter we will examine these various religious groups or positions that emphasize the imminent end of the world.

References

1. Hal Lindsey, *The Late Great Planet Earth* (Grand Rapids: Zondervan Publishing House, 1970).
2. *Time,* March 5, 1979.
3. William E. Biederwolf, *The Second Coming Bible* (Grand Rapids: Baker Book House, 1972).
4. William Willoughby, *The Washington Evening Star,* June 30, 1973.
5. Leslie H. Woodson, *Population, Pollution, and Prophecy* (Old

MODERN INTEREST IN THE END OF THE WORLD

Tappan, N.J.: Fleming H. Revell Company, 1973).
Richard DeHaan, *Israel and the Nations of Prophecy* (Grand Rapids: Zondervan Publishing House, 1971).
Guy Duty, *Christ's Coming and the World Church* (Minneapolis: Bethany Fellowship Inc., 1971).
Tim LaHaye, *The Beginning of the End* (Wheaton, Ill.: Tyndale House Publishers, 1972).
Robert H. Gundry, *The Church and the Tribulation* (Grand Rapids: Zondervan Publishing House, 1973).

6. George Wald, Nobel Prize-winning biologist, Harvard University, in "Earth Doomed, Scientist Contends," Louisville *Courier-Journal*, February 5, 1970; Wayne H. Davis, *Archives of Environmental Health*, July 1970, p. 4.

7. Donella H. Meadows, et al, *The Limits to Growth* (New York: Signet, 1972).

8. *Atlas World Press Review*, January 1979.

9. Herman Kahn, a name almost synonymous the world over with "think tank" and future scenarios, is described in the December 1975 issue of *The Futurist* as "the unthinkable optimist." He is depicted as one who "labors under the burden of being an optimist in a period when pessimism is more fashionable in intellectual circles. To the horror of many, he is convinced that the years ahead will probably be good for most people." In that same issue, Kahn rather convincingly argues that "despite its many problems, the world now enjoys a higher standard of living than ever before and its future looks bright." He answers "Absolutely not" to such questions as Are we running out of energy, natural resources, or food? And "Absolutely yes" to the questions Can we retain clean air and water? He ends his article: "All in all, we remain optimistic about the potential of man's future. We can only hope that he does not throw away this potential through foolish political behaviour or misplaced concern about nonexistent or badly formulated growth issues." Page 334.

10. *San Jose Mercury*, January 29, 1979.

11. *Christianity Today*, February 2, 1979, p. 18.

12. Alexander Solzhenitsyn, *The Gulag Archipelago* (New York: Harper & Row, Publishers, 1973).

13. *Time*, June 19, 1978, p. 33.

14. *National Review*, July 7, 1978.

15. *Ibid.*

16. Leon J. Wood, *The Bible and Future Events* (Grand Rapids: Zondervan Publishing House, 1973), p. 19.

17. John F. Walvoord with John E. Walvoord, *Armageddon* (Grand Rapids: Zondervan Publishing House, 1974), p. 39.

18. *Ibid.*, p. 73.

19. *Ibid.*, p. 207.

Conflicting Doctrines of the Second Advent

In this chapter we will examine briefly a number of conflicting doctrines of the second advent. We will review three viewpoints often included under the term "liberal" theology, three positions held among those generally known as "conservative" theologians, and the Seventh-day Adventist teaching regarding the return of Jesus and the end of the world.

INTERPRETATIONS OF LIBERAL THEOLOGIANS

Generally speaking, liberal theologians (those who do not accept, among other matters, the biblical text as the inerrant expression of the will of God and the Christian's infallible guide to faith and practice) interpret biblical passages referring to a second coming of Jesus as (1) being fulfilled in the biblical writer's time; as (2) examples of contemporary apocalypticisms[1] that carried no authentic predictive value; or as (3) a basis for a revolutionary principle that eventually shapes the future of this present world only. None of these three representative schools envisages a literal return of the historical Jesus.

C. H. Dodd, British Congregational minister and New Testament scholar, has been the leading modern proponent of the concept known as "realized eschatology." Dodd taught that the Christian church gradually realized that the decisive hour for the world *had* come in the person of Jesus Christ, that, in Him, the "eternal" had decisively entered history. In his book *The Parables of the Kingdom*[2] Dodd contended that while Jesus used apocalyptic symbolisms to emphasize the absolute otherness of the kingdom of God, He used parables to illustrate the idea that the kingdom of God had indeed come, then and there. Dodd himself believed in a final coming of Christ, but not within history as we know it.

CONFLICTING DOCTRINES OF THE SECOND ADVENT

We cannot agree with Dodd and others (e.g. James A. T. Robinson's "inaugurated eschatology"³) who believe that the New Testament doctrine of the advent can be reduced to a twofold postulate: (1) Christ comes whenever a person firmly believes in His first coming and resurrection and (2) that all mankind will eventually be united and taken up into God beyond history (universalism).

Representing the second school of liberal thought is Albert Schweitzer—German theologian, medical missionary, and musician—who was the first to advocate what has been labeled "consistent" or "thoroughgoing" eschatology. In this position, Jesus mistakenly understood Himself to be the "Coming One." Since the end did not come as He and His disciples had hoped, Christians today must de-eschatologize the New Testament (that is, cleanse the New Testament of any literal, Heaven-initiated end to this world.)⁴

Schweitzer and his followers, however, never presented a convincing explanation for (1) the rise of the Christian church that was supposedly built on a Leader who had been deceived by His own theology and for (2) the courage and joy of His early followers who survived this crushing disappointment.

Rudolf Bultmann, one of the major New Testament scholars of the twentieth century, also emphasized the decisive character of Christ's death and resurrection as Dodd did but followed Schweitzer with a more radical position. He taught that John, especially, dismissed the futuristic aspect of eschatology, reducing all "adventist hope" to the present, existential event of Christ as He appears in the decision of faith. For Bultmann the act of faith, knowing Christ in one's personal existence, is the Christian's decisive event.⁵ All references to a literal return of Jesus and to an end to this world are pure myth:

"The *mythical eschatology* is untenable for the simple reason that the parousia of Christ never took place as the New Testament expected. History did not come to an end, and, as every schoolboy knows, it will continue to run its course. Even if we believe that the world as we know it will come to an end in time, we expect the end to take the form of a natural catastrophe, not of a mythical event such as the New Testament expects."[6]

Bultmann's followers have been many. The demythologizers flowing broadly out of the Bultmann school have dissolved the literality of the New Testament advent passages, even as earlier and more traditional liberals had, although using different reasons. The end result is the same: no prophetic assistance in determining the nature and time of the literal return of Jesus and of the end of the world.

Even though Bultmann rightly emphasizes the crucial nature of Christian decision here and now, he gives away too much. He denudes the New Testament of one of its main themes—the Christian hope that one day good will triumph over evil—finally and irrevocably—by a specific, particular, historical act of God. He failed to see how this advent principle, coupled with his faith-existential theme, would add to his concern for Christian urgency and ethical motivation.

The third major grouping of liberal interpretations regarding the New Testament emphasis on "end times" and the second advent centers in a relatively recent development referred to by such terms as "theology of liberation," "theology of hope," or "theology of revolution."

Scholars such as Jurgen Moltmann[7] and Carl E. Braaten stress that eschatological hope sows a theology of social revolution. Braaten states that the authentic preaching of the gospel unlooses a revolutionary assault on all societal structures that are antichristian and that "Christians are to form a peace corps of God's kingdom in the world, an army of salvation signalling 'the way' to a future in which violence will be no more, and 'there shall be an end to death, and to mourning and crying and pain.' That is the final goal of the revolutionary existence of the Christians in the world."[8]

The advocates of the "theology of the liberation" reject a literal interpretation of the second advent texts in favor of a "here and now" application. They understand the "new world" texts to describe the end result of Christian perseverance, using whatever tactics necessary, in establishing on this earth a world society free from oppression for all people. Some call this approach the politicizing of the gospel.

CONFLICTING DOCTRINES OF THE SECOND ADVENT

A practical example of how the liberal positions affect the life of the church was seen in the Inaugural Symposium (1973) at Seabury-Western Theological Seminary, honoring the seminary's new president and dean, Arman Jorjorian. The symposium's theme was "the future," and it featured Robert Theobald, a well-known futurologist.

Theobald reportedly contended that "the answer to the future is not destructive revolution but constructive evolution, through such changes as the guaranteed income, the blending of work and leisure, the creation of larger social units than the 'nuclear family' and the development of new dwelling patterns suitable for these units (such as modifications of the Navaho 'hogan'). We must take the *Whole Earth Catalog* seriously when it says, 'We are gods and we might as well get good at it.' "[9]

The interesting fact is that a Christian seminary "could hold a symposium on the future without once mentioning the return of our Lord Jesus Christ to judge the quick and the dead."[10]

INTERPRETATIONS OF CONSERVATIVE THEOLOGIANS

When we turn to conservative theologians and churches, Christendom is even more fragmented. Conservatives are divided into at least three main groups—nonmillennialists (or amillennialists), postmillennialists, and premillennialists—and then into divisions within these groups.

The nonmillennialist (sometimes called amillennialist) believes no scriptural ground exists for expecting a literal millennium (a 1000-year period between the first and second resurrections). Because most nonmillennialists are Lutherans and Calvinists and thus believe in the conscious state of the dead (either in heaven or hell), they experience inner conflict over mention of a resurrection. Nonmillennialists do not teach that both resurrections (good and bad) are physical, although for some the second is physical. Although many nonmillennialists believe that Jesus will return literally, it is more than interesting that few, if any, are found among the voices proclaiming the nearness of the advent. Among twentieth-century exponents of nonmillennialism,

THE END: THE UNIQUE VOICE OF ADVENTISTS

although with varying emphases, are L. Berkhof, A. Kuyper, G. Bos, G. C. Berkouwer, and E. P. Clowney. Nonmillennialists are often grouped with postmillennialists, probably because some were the latter and changed their opinions as world conditions deteriorated in the twentieth century. Also, nonmillennialists usually make a point of distinguishing themselves from a premillennial position more readily than they seem to differentiate from postmillennialism.

POSTMILLENNIALISM

Postmillennialists hold that the return of Jesus *follows* the millennial period predicted in Revelation 20. During this time, in their view, the gospel will have been generally accepted throughout the world, ushering in a golden age of prosperity and well-being. One group within postmillennialists has believed that the Holy Spirit is the effective agent that gradually brings a global triumph over the powers of evil. Such theologians as Augustine, Jonathan Edwards, Benjamin B. Warfield, and A. H. Strong have advocated this view, although Augustine and Warfield have been claimed also by the nonmillennialists.

Adam Clarke, a Methodist scholar and author of the perennially famous *Clarke's Commentary,* reflected a strong nineteenth-century-postmillennialist position. In his comments on the 1000-year period in Revelation 20, he wrote:

"This . . . no doubt refers to a time in which the influence of Satan will be greatly restrained, and the true Church of God enjoy great prosperity, which shall endure for a long time. But it is not likely that the number, a thousand years, is to be taken literally here, and *year* symbolically and figuratively in all the book beside. . . . There is no doubt that the earth is in a state of progressive moral improvement; and that the light of true religion is shining . . . more and more to the perfect day. But *when* the religion of Christ will be at its meridian of light and heat, we know not. . . . Probably no such a time shall ever appear, in which evil shall be wholly banished from the earth, till after the day of judgment, when the earth having been burnt up, a new heaven and a new

CONFLICTING DOCTRINES OF THE SECOND ADVENT

earth shall be produced out of the ruins of the old, by the mighty power of God."[11]

Seventh-day Adventists, a century ago, had to contend with the forceful presentations of postmillennialists. James White's first chapter in *Bible Adventism*, "The Millennium," was a forthright answer to postmillennialism when it was extremely popular.[12]

Another postmillennial group (often merging with theological liberalism) rejects the supernatural intervention of the Holy Spirit as the causative agent that ushers in the golden age of a world free from the blight of ignorance and sin. Its hopes rest in the evolutionary process whereby the principles of Jesus, such as set forth in the Sermon on the Mount, will gradually be adopted by increasingly wiser men and women as time goes on. Representatives of this position would include William Newton Clarke, William Adams Brown, Walter Rauschenbusch, and Shailer Matthews. However, the events of the twentieth century have shaken out such optimism among biblical expositors, and rarely does one find such triumphal optimism today.[13]

Although postmillennialism has been relatively mute for decades there seems to be a revival, especially among Reformed scholars such as Norman Shephard, R. J. Rushdoony, and Gary North.

Loraine Boettner expects the world substantially to be converted before Jesus returns, ushering in a long period of earthly peace (the millennium is not necessarily 1000 years). At the end of the millennial peace there will be an apostasy and a revival of evil, reminding everyone of how terrible sin truly is. The crisis ends with the visible return of Jesus.[14]

J. Marcellus Kik outlined a postmillennial eschatology, *An Eschatology of Victory*. Dividing his ideas into three parts, Kik reviewed the spiritual lineage of postmillennialism (especially highlighting the classic reformers); interpreted Matthew 24 as being fulfilled in the first century; and analyzed Revelation 20 (the millennium chapter), viewing the New Jerusalem as part of the present Messianic kingdom with the gospel progressing around the world—separating it from the kingdom of glory that will follow the return of Jesus.[15]

THE END: THE UNIQUE VOICE OF ADVENTISTS

PREMILLENNIALISM

When we turn to the premillennialists (those who believe that Jesus will literally return prior to the 1000-year period of Revelation 20), we enter a complex area, a jungle thicket. Although there are three main divisions of premillennialists —pretribulationists, posttribulationists, and Seventh-day Adventists—the first two divisions have fragmented into a variety of distinctive positions.

Pretribulationists believe that before Jesus returns visibly and the millennial reign of the saints begins, He will come secretly *for His church*. This "coming" and the subsequent snatching of the saints to heaven is called the "secret rapture."[16] A seven-year period (the seventieth week of Daniel 9:27) follows the "rapture," during which the Jews are converted and the antichrist revealed amidst a time of great tribulation. Some contend that during this period Russia and China will converge on Palestine and in this titanic struggle, China will destroy Russia.

At the end of this seven-year period Christ *returns with His saints* (in glory and visible to all on earth), resurrects the saved who died during the seven-year period, destroys the antichrist, and binds Satan. The temple is restored in literal Jerusalem, becoming Christ's headquarters on earth, thus beginning the millennial rule on earth.

With interesting variations, this "secret rapture" motif has been set forth most forcefully in the Scofield Bible, by the Plymouth Brethren, and by many seminaries and Bible institutes.[17] Some very committed Christians, including R. A. Torrey, Harry A. Ironside, Louis T. Talbot, A. C. Gaebelein, L. Nelson Bell, Charles C. Ryrie, John Walvoord, E. Schuyler English, C. M. Ward, Charles L. Feinberg, Richard DeHaan, Martin DeHaan, Donald Barnhouse, L. S. Chafer, Henry Thiessen, Wilbur M. Smith, and C. H. Mackintosh (CHM) have taught this position, though they may differ in some details.

Posttribulationists differ from the pretribulationists chiefly by denying a secret rapture of the church;[18] in most other respects they agree with the pretrib advocates in such

CONFLICTING DOCTRINES OF THE SECOND ADVENT

areas as believing the Jewish state to be a fulfillment of last-day prophecy and in reserving for the future immediately preceding the advent the seventieth week of Daniel 9 and the events of Revelation chapters 4 to 19. During this period the antichrist would be revealed and the great tribulation of the church unleashed.

Over the past twenty-five years a growing tendency has emerged on the part of younger premillenarians to join the posttrib advocates. Spokesmen for this group, though differing in some respects, include George Ladd, Edward J. Carnell, Norman Douty, Bernard Ramm, Harold Ockenga, Peter Beyerhaus, R. H. Gundry, and David McPherson. Even though this swing to a posttrib position among premillennialists has been viewed as a rising revolt,[19] it has not been a swing to the historic Adventist position, which also has been traditionally opposed to the pretribulation position. Neither has it muted the remarkable impact of the pretribulationists as television, radio, books, magazines, and the neighborhood theater combine to grip the attention and dazzle the imagination of the present generation with the secret-rapture viewpoint.

As these lines are being written, local television stations are saturating the United States with vivid, awesome, spot advertisements directing viewers to see the film version of *The Late Great Planet Earth*,[20] Hal Lindsey's runaway bestseller. The book has already sold more than ten million copies—and now the film.

HAL LINDSEY'S ARGUMENT

Because of its obvious appeal and high visibility, an examination of Lindsey's argument may be helpful. Applying the words "This generation will not pass away till all these things take place" (Matthew 24:34), Lindsey believes that the end of the world will come within the lifetime of the generation that saw the founding of the Israeli state in 1948.

He views the recapture of old Jersalem in 1967 as another significant and necessary event in the rapidly culminating movements of prophetic fulfillment. The next and final step that would indicate the imminence of Christ's return is for

THE END: THE UNIQUE VOICE OF ADVENTISTS

Israel to rebuild the ancient temple on its old site because, as Lindsey believes, Jesus predicted that the temple would be standing and would suffer sacrilege immediately prior to His return.

Lindsey sees the image of Daniel 2 and the beasts of Daniel 7 as the great outline of world history, culminating in the reemergence of the ancient Roman Empire confederacy through the setting up of ten nations (ten horns) that will eventually form the European Common Market.

He contends that Russia is the mighty force of the north spoken of in Ezekiel 38 and 39 that will finally attack Israel. However, Russia will eventually be destroyed by an event so extraordinary that the Jews will recognize it as the intervention of God, opening the way for many Jews to be converted to Jesus, the true Messiah.

China, for Lindsey, after unifying the kings of the east, will assemble a vast war machine that will one day bring on the battle of Armageddon.

Lindsey believes that Rome will be the seat of the religiopolitical world leader, or "future führer," who rises at the time of world anarchy and distress with a bewitching plan and charm to save the world from total destruction. After making an alliance with the Jews, this religious leader will move his world headquarters from Rome to Jerusalem.

When God concludes that the time is ripe, He will snatch away His living church ("secret rapture"). The ensuing seven years will be the worst period of famine, bloodshed, and ghastly pestilence that this world has ever known. During the great tribulation the focus will be on God's dealing with the Jews, who again are given the responsibility for the evangelization of the world.

At the end of the seven-year or great-tribulation period, at the climax of Armageddon, when mankind is about ready to incinerate the world, Jesus returns gloriously and saves mankind from self-extinction. At that time Jesus will set up a literal millennial reign on earth, with Jerusalem functioning as the spiritual capital of the world.

There are two basic mistakes in Lindsey's reasoning: He is confused regarding (1) the "secret rapture" and (2) the im-

CONFLICTING DOCTRINES OF THE SECOND ADVENT

portance of the modern Jewish nation in last-day events.

THE FALLACY OF THE SECRET-RAPTURE THEORY

The entrenchment of the secret-rapture theory within evangelical Protestantism, although not universal, is a relatively modern phenomenon. Proponents of this position seem to dominate evangelical prophetic conferences and most evangelical periodicals. To the uninformed, this predominant evangelical position appears to be the traditional teaching of the Christian church since New Testament days. Nothing is further from the truth.

The concept of the secret rapture was not conceived before the early 1830s when, in England, a woman of Edward Irving's congregation, thinking herself under some kind of charismatic gift, announced her "new light." Hard as it is to believe, several scholars of the famous Powerscourt meetings (much to the protest of their colleagues) advocated this new position as an important ingredient in their developing outline of a new brand of premillennialism.[21] It seemed to be the incentive that two other struggling ideas needed: (1) futurism, the concept that the seventieth week of Daniel 9 and the prophecies of Revelation 4 to 22 were yet future events to be completed during the seven years immediately preceding the return of Jesus in judgment and (2) Darby's dispensationalism. Dispensationalism not only denied to the Christian church its traditional role as the successor to the Jewish nation, but also looked forward to the final gospel call to be given by the Jews after the faithful Christians had been "raptured."

The main support for the secret-rapture doctrine has come from the Plymouth Brethren movement, the Scofield Reference Bible, seminaries such as the Dallas Theological Seminary and Biola plus many Bible institutes and colleges. Perhaps the chief reason for the rapid acceptance of pretribulationism during the past 100 years was that its emphasis on the nearness of Christ's return seemed, to evangelical Christians, to be the most effective weapon against postmillennialism, the overwhelming prophetic interpretation during the optimistic nineteenth century. The secret-rapture teaching seemed to recover the authentic New Testament emphasis on imminence and, for many Christians looking for the return of Jesus, this restored a sense of realism that had long been lost.

But much was conceded and lost while recovering imminence. Up until the 1830s, Bible students generally since apostolic times had located the glorification of the church at the time when Jesus returns in glory. The dispensationalists (those who separate the seventieth week of Daniel 7 and the prophecies of Revelation 4 to 22 from their historical context), employing the secret rapture concept, have placed the translation of the living church seven years before the visible return of Jesus. Among the reasons for this "late" discovery in prophetic interpretation are that (1) they do not envision the church going through the great tribulation, (2) they see no other way for the Jews to be responsible for the final gospel call to the world, and (3) they believe that the saints will have to be translated before our Lord's visible return in order to satisfy Paul's statement that Jesus would return "with all his saints." 1 Thessalonians 3:13.

By an amazing and intricate system of textual maneuvering the Bible is tortured into making distinctions between the undifferentiable and forced into assertions that are mere assumptions and not developed out of the biblical text.[22]

For example, three words in the Greek are used to describe our Lord's return: *parousia* "coming," *apokalupsis* "uncovering, revelation," and *epiphaneia* "manifestation, appearance." *Parousia* is used by secret-rapture advocates to refer to Christ's secret coming for His church, while the remaining two words are reserved for His visible return after the seven-year tribulation period.

But one of many examples where *parousia* is used in connection with the advent is 1 Thessalonians 4:15-17: "For this we declare to you by the word of the Lord, that we who are alive, who are left until the coming [*parousia*] of the Lord, shall not precede those who have fallen asleep. For the Lord himself will descend from heaven with a cry of command, with the archangel's call, and with the sound of the trumpet of God. And the dead in Christ will rise first; then we

CONFLICTING DOCTRINES OF THE SECOND ADVENT

who are alive, who are left, shall be caught up together with them in the clouds to meet the Lord in the air; and so we shall always be with the Lord."

It takes great ingenuity to find a secret rapture amid shouts and trumpets loud enough to awaken the dead! The living saints are joined with Jesus only after the dead in Jesus are raised. Nothing seems to be quiet, hidden, or secret in this verse or any other verse where *parousia* is used in reference to the second advent.

Paul expected the church to remain on earth until the visible revelation (*apokalupsis*) of Jesus (1 Corinthians 1:7), urging the church to keep its eye on "that blessed hope, and the glorious appearing (*epiphaneia*) of the great God and our Saviour Jesus Christ." Titus 2:13, K.J.V. These three Greek words describe the same event, a single event, that will occur at the end of a great time of trouble. Paul knew nothing other than that the Christian saints will be on earth, amid the awfulness of the great time of trouble and the outpouring of the wrath of God, until Jesus descends "with power and great glory." Matthew 24:30.

Secret-rapture advocates insist that the church must be raptured before the great tribulation, chiefly because they had already decided that the seventieth week of Daniel 9 must include both this seven-year period as just preceding the visible return of Jesus and a restored Jewish nation targeted for the antichrist's wrath. Regardless of the fact that the New Testament always envisions the church as a living participant of the last, great time of trouble (suffering the wrath of men, but not of God), dispensationalists cut short the age of the church at the beginning of the seventieth week, allowing for the resumption of the age of Israel so that the Old Testament prophecies concerning the restoration of Israel might be fulfilled.

Historically, however, prophetic interpreters (as do Seventh-day Adventists today) have kept the seventieth week of Daniel 9:24-27 integrated with the 70-week (490-year) prophecy, beginning in 457 B.C. and ending in A.D. 34.[23]

Contrary also to the pretribulationists, the Bible says nothing to support the idea that the resurrection of the righteous

THE END: THE UNIQUE VOICE OF ADVENTISTS

occurs in two phases—at the beginning and at the end of the seven-year period (with people converted during the period of Jewish evangelism, then martyred and resurrected at the latter end). Revelation 20 speaks categorically about only two resurrections, that of the righteous at the beginning of the millennium and that of the unrighteous at the end of the millennium.

Seventh-day Adventists believe that the Bible should be read in a straightforward manner. The Bible was not meant to be a puzzle. Unquestionably, there are difficult passages, but Adventists contend, as serious Bible students have always held, that the simplest explanation is preferable to the complicated and strained, that the burden of proof rests upon those who advocate a doctrine that the Bible does not explicitly teach.

The fact that pretribulationists have modified their positions many times over the years, that many leading advocates have abandoned this position after more careful Bible study, should suggest that the secret-rapture position rests on precarious footing, even for its friends. But it surely makes dramatic motion pictures!

THE FALLACY OF ISRAEL AS A LAST-DAY KEY

The second fundamental error in Hal Lindsey's *The Late Great Planet Earth,* and the pretribulation position in general, is the insistence that the establishment of the modern state of Israel strongly indicates that the return of Jesus is near.

Hal Lindsey wrote, "Some time in the future there will be a seven-year period climaxed by the visible return of Jesus Christ. . . . The general time of this seven-year period couldn't begin until the Jewish people re-established their nation in their ancient homeland of Palestine. . . . The one event which many Bible students in the past overlooked was this paramount prophetic sign: Israel had to be a nation again in the land of its forefathers. . . . The same prophets who predicted the world-wide exile and persecution of the Jews also predicted their restoration as a nation. It is surprising that many could not see the obvious: since the first part of

CONFLICTING DOCTRINES OF THE SECOND ADVENT

these prophecies came true we should have anticipated that the second part would come true, also. This restoration was to come about in the general time of the climactic seven-year countdown and its finale—the personal appearance of the Messiah to deliver the new state from destruction. . . .

"To be specific about Israel's great significance as a sign of the time, there are three things that were to happen. First, the Jewish nation would be reborn in the land of Palestine. Secondly, the Jews would repossess old Jerusalem and the sacred sites. Thirdly, they would rebuild their ancient temple of worship upon its historic site."[24]

Lindsey liberally quotes Old Testament prophets, Matthew 24, and Romans 9 to 11 to support this viewpoint, as do dozens of popular broadcasters and authors of a dizzying number of books and magazine articles.

How can so many Bible interpreters believe that the modern state of Israel is a dramatic fulfillment of prophecy when Seventh-day Adventists and such scholars as J. Barton Payne[25] see no prophetic significance in the new Jewish state? The reason is simple: When Bible students overlook the principle of conditional prophecy, only havoc ensues, not only in understanding Israel's role and mission, but in other subjects as well. (The biblical principle of conditional prophecy will be discussed in our next chapter.)

Because of this misunderstanding of conditional prophecy several specific errors developed that have been crucial and tragic to the Christian church. Probably the greatest mistake is known as dispensationalism (referred to earlier in this chapter). The crux of this very popular evangelical position is that the Christian church is not to be understood as the bearer of the responsibilities once given to the Jews; the Christian church is only one phase (a parenthesis) in a sequence of dispensations as God works out His plan for man. The Jews, for the dispensationalist, will yet enjoy literally all the Old Testament promises and blessings, with Jerusalem becoming the spiritual center of the world during the millennium. (In our next chapter we will examine this error more fully.)

It seems evident that if the relationship of Israel and the

45

THE END: THE UNIQUE VOICE OF ADVENTISTS

Christian church had been correctly understood, Daniel 9 need not have been forced into a gap theory placing the Christian age between two Jewish dispensations, nor would any need exist to invent the secret-rapture theory (neatly removing Christians from the earth in order to make Jews again the focal point of God's activity as His final evangelists to the world). The whole dispensationalist argument, and thus, for all practical purposes, the Israel-restoration syndrome, rests upon a faulty understanding of the nature of the Christian church.

In fact, John F. Walvoord, president of Dallas Theological Seminary and probably the leading spokesman for the secret rapture, pretribulation position, wrote: "It is therefore not too much to say that the rapture question is determined more by ecclesiology than eschatology. . . . It is safe to say that pretribulationism depends upon a particular definition of the church, and any consideration of pretribulationism which does not take this major factor into consideration will be largely beside the point."[26]

The issue thus is clear: Begin with biblical exegesis, and no support will be found for the secret-rapture theory, with its seven years of tribulation and the rebuilding of the temple in Jerusalem. But if one begins with the presupposition that the Christian church was not given the task of being God's instrument of grace after the Jews rejected Christ, then, very contrived exegesis would be required whereby clear, explicit texts are tortured beyond recognition.

Seventh-day Adventists believe that chief among the reasons why the modern state of Israel has no prophetic significance is that after the Jews rejected Jesus as the Messiah, God gave to the Christian church the special privileges, responsibilities, and prerogatives once assigned to the ancient Jews. No longer were the Jews to be His special people with a prophetic destiny.

As soon as the secret-rapture proponents concede (1) that the Christian church, composed of both Jew and Gentile, was given the same commission once given to the Jewish people—that is, to proclaim the good news of salvation through faith in the Messiah—and (2) that nevermore as a

CONFLICTING DOCTRINES OF THE SECOND ADVENT

people would the Jews be a special evangelistic instrument in the plan of salvation, then the pretribulation position will disintegrate.

Dr. Walvoord recognizes this crucial point well: "The doctrine of the church has been rightly considered by theologians of all points of view as being an integral and important aspect of theology as a whole. Systems of theology can often be characterized by their ecclesiology. The premillennial system of interpretation has especially relied upon a proper understanding of the doctrine of the church as a body distinct from Israel and from saints in general. What is essential to premillennialism becomes an indispensable foundation in the study of pretribulationism."[27]

Walvoord continues: "Any answer to the rapture question must therefore be based upon a careful study of the doctrine of the church as it is revealed in the New Testament. To a large extent premillennialism is dependent upon the definition of the church, and premillenarians who fail to distinguish between Israel and the church erect their structure of premillennial doctrine on a weak foundation."[28]

The deciding issue could not have been better said: Walvoord is correct when he says that the whole issue of the secret rapture rests on his interpretation of what constitutes the "church." But Walvoord is wrong when he attempts to distinguish (1) between the responsibilities given by God to the Jewish nation prior to the cross and those given to the Christian church; and (2) between the "church" that will be raptured and all other Christians before and after the rapture.

The awesome Matterhorn truth of the New Testament is that there is no spiritual distinction between the men of faith in the Old Testament and the men of faith in the New.

"So you see that it is men of faith who are the sons of Abraham. And the scripture, foreseeing that God would justify the Gentiles by faith, preached the gospel beforehand to Abraham, saying, 'In thee shall all the nations be blessed.' So then, those who are men of faith are blessed with Abraham who had faith . . . for in Christ Jesus you are all sons of God, through faith. And if you are Christ's then you are Abraham's offspring, heirs according to promise." Galatians 3:7-9, 26, 29.

THE END: THE UNIQUE VOICE OF ADVENTISTS

The earliest Christians were Jews. These Jewish Christians were founders of an organization that had one primary objective—to proclaim that their Lord Jesus was the Messiah, the world's Saviour, who saves His followers from both the penalty and power of sin.

This postcross message was essentially no different from what clear-eyed prophets had been saying before Calvary. Men of genuine faith are saved from the power and penalty of sin—whether they lived before the cross as Jews or after the cross as Christians. But after the cross the message became clearer and man's rebellion less excusable.

No place is found in the New Testament for the dispensationalist distinction between the "church" (with its distinctive and specific time period in the plan of salvation) and "Israel" (with its two time periods as God's special people separated by the "church's" dispensation).

In regard to Walvoord's attempt to distinguish between the "raptured" saints and those Christians who are alive at the dramatic, glorious, visible return of Jesus, it should be noted that the New Testament nowhere recognizes the emergence of an elite class of Christians who will be snatched to heaven prior to the great seven-year tribulation.

Although Adventists assign no prophetical importance to the establishment of modern Israel, they do place a high theological significance upon the existence of the Jewish race, a people rich with history and responsibility, who have greatly enriched all nations. They are a standing object lesson of God's prophetic words pronounced in Deuteronomy; yet, God seems to be saying, even today, "Israel, I still want you to come to me."[29]

ADVENTISTS ARE CLASSIC HISTORICISTS

Although Seventh-day Adventists are premillennialists, they do not see prophetic importance in the establishment of the Jewish state in 1948, or the annexation of Old Jerusalem in 1967; neither do they accept the principle of futurism which assigns the seventieth week of Daniel 7 to a future seven-year period just prior to Christ's return. At the same time, Adventists reject the imminence emphasis (that Jesus

CONFLICTING DOCTRINES OF THE SECOND ADVENT

can come this very day) because there are several aspects of prophecy—such as the national Sunday law and the seven last plagues—that must be fulfilled before Jesus will return. Nearness of the advent—about this there is no doubt. But imminence in the sense of "at any moment," no. A gifted writer wrote: "You will not be able to say that He will come in one, two, or five years, neither are you to put off His coming by stating that it may not be for ten or twenty years. It is the duty of the people of God to have their lamps trimmed and burning, to be as men that wait for the Bridegroom, when He shall return from the wedding."[30]

Adventists, furthermore, view the millennium not as a glorious reign by Christ on earth with Jerusalem as His capital, but as an intermediate period between the first and second resurrections when the redeemed are with the Lord "in heaven" and the earth is desolate. No other church seems to hold this view.

Basically Adventists teach the classic, historical position advocated in principle by many of the church fathers and most of the Reformers. Such a position combines certain aspects of the preterist, historicist, and futurist interpretations. Elements in Daniel and the Revelation, for example, were fulfilled during the time of the Bible writers; other portions were fulfilled with the breakup of the Roman Empire and the subsequent reign of the papacy; yet other elements of prophecy are still future in their application. But in assigning some elements of prophecy to a yet future date, Seventh-day Adventists do not fall into the fallacy of pre- or post-tribulationists who require, for example, a seven-year period of tribulation and/or the emergence of Israel as a significant last-day sign.

The main embarrassment of most premillennialists is that their cry of imminence has become a victim of the credibility gap. At the Jerusalem Conference on Biblical Prophecy in 1972, Wilbur M. Smith, an eminent evangelical, said, "In discussing this subject of the 'signs of the times' we must be exceedingly careful not to assert dogmatically that because of this condition and that we *must* be at the end of the age. This identification of contemporary events, as indicating the

THE END: THE UNIQUE VOICE OF ADVENTISTS

imminence of the end of the age, is a subject that has produced enormous literature down through the ages. One can gather a whole library of books in which events when taking place are set forth as tokens of the end of time."[31]

Dr. Smith amplified his thought by giving examples of the hazards of interpreting contemporary events: "In the early church it was generally believed that the fall of the Roman Empire meant the end of the age. Thus, Tertullian's *Apology* declared, 'We know that a mighty shock is impending over the whole earth—in fact, the very end of all things threatening dreadful war—is only retarded by the continued existence of the Roman Empire.' But Rome fell, and the Lord did not come.

"Perhaps it will not be out of order to quote here . . . a remarkable statement by Martin Luther on Luke's account of the Olivet discourse: 'I do not wish to force or constrain any one to believe as I do; but neither will I permit any one, on the other hand, to take from me my belief that the day of judgment is not far off. Christ's words and these signs move me so to believe; for whatever chronicles we may read, from the time of Christ until now, we shall not find a parallel to what the world has shown itself within the present century. Such building and planting has never been so common—so universal; such expensive and varied food; and drinks have also never been so usual as in our day. To such an extravagance of expense have people also gone for clothing as to make it impossible to go any futher; and who has ever read of such commercial operations as are now encircling and swallowing up the world? Whilst all descriptions of art and science are coming up, and have come up, the like of which has never been since Christ was born.

" 'The world has reached its very culmination in what relates to temporal interests, or what Christ calls, "the care of this life," eating, drinking, building, planting, buying, selling, marrying, doing for children, and such like, which, whosoever considers, must acknowledge that it cannot hold much longer.'

"All this more than four hundred years ago!

"At the beginning of the nineteenth century there was

CONFLICTING DOCTRINES OF THE SECOND ADVENT

considerable literature insisting that Napoleon Bonaparte was the antichrist, and even larger literature, a few years later, claiming that Napoleon III was the antichrist. Indeed, such a careful student as Dr. Ironside, in his booklet *Looking Backward Over a Third of a Century of Prophetic Fulfillment* (1930) devoted three pages to the significance of Mussolini, when we now know that Mussolini had no prophetic significance at all. Even Dr. Scofield, in his volume *Addresses on Prophecy*, first published in 1900, gave it as his opinion that the world was preparing for a great world war which would be the last war and which would usher in the King of kings. Well, the Great War came, and then in a few years the Second World War, and now we talk easily about World War III, on which we will have more to say later—but these have not ushered in the King.

"A century ago, in 1863, in the first volume of what was to become a famous prophetic journal *The Prophetic Times*, we find the following statement which proved to be an inaccurate interpretation of conditions then prevailing: 'surveying, then, this excited, exciting, and threatening state of things the world over,—the multitudes of men engaged in deadly strife, and the multitudes more in arms and at the command of leaders preparing to give the word which at any moment may make the vast world one field of blood,—the fearful activity of agencies and elements which have been the deprecation of wise and good men of all ages,—the disintegration, revolution, impiety, selfishness, and treachery, enfeebling and destroying all the fabrics and ties by which society has hitherto been preserved,—and a cunning, ambitious, and unprincipled adventurer, leagued with revolution, rising to the head of earthly power, and promising the world liberty and peace by means of his own universal, despotic dictatorship, which troubled and restless peoples seem at any time ready to accept,—what conclusion can we draw, but that unexampled changes are at hand, and that all that Christ and his prophets have spoken respecting the last perilous times, and the Man of Sin, are about to have their speedy fulfillment?' . . .

"We must be very careful in discussing signs of our Lord's

THE END: THE UNIQUE VOICE OF ADVENTISTS

return not to introduce some of the amazing things that are going on in our world just because they are exciting, or remarkable, or even profoundly influential. The projection of various missiles and photographing equipment into the sky, and letting them continue to encircle our globe, has no relation to prophecy at all. Even our landing on the moon has no connection with the *prophecies* regarding the darkening of the moon."[32]

Perhaps some Adventist preachers can recall their early years when they were admonished to preach that World War I—and later World War II—was surely Armageddon, that Turkey was the "key" to last-day events, that she would come to her end with none to help her, thus fulfilling Daniel 11, or that the crisis over oil in the Middle East would lead to a military conflict called Armageddon—and how the list could be multiplied.

Nevertheless, even though individual Adventists from time to time have made unwarranted assumptions regarding what they thought were specific signs of the end (thereby embarrassing themselves and adding to the credibility gap), mainline Seventh-day Adventist theology is not embarrassed by the current dilemma shared by others who have proclaimed a literal return of Jesus and the establishment of the kingdom of glory within the context of the secret rapture and the seven-year-tribulation/return-of-Israel position.

Typical of the evangelical embarrassment regarding "end of the world" predictions are the following comments selected at random. After reviewing seven recently published books on eschatology, Bob Ross noted, "After finishing this seven-course prophetic meal, I am not sure whether I merely feel stuffed or am suffering from some indigestion. . . . In the first place, I feel concern that so much evangelical material published in this field [eschatology] is rather simplistic and unreflective. Each author has his own preconceived doctrinal stance and simply goes from that point. . . . Despite constant reminders of the importance of a literal interpretation often the author's theological bias prevents him from letting the Bible speak for itself in terms of its own concerns expressed in its unique historical circumstances. . . .

CONFLICTING DOCTRINES OF THE SECOND ADVENT

"I have been forced to ask why we are having so much trouble coming up with a mutually agreeable interpretation of the last things. For example, among the books reviewed here there are at least two totally different interpretations of Matthew 24 and as many significant variations as there are commentators. When it comes to some doctrine like Christology or soteriology, evangelicals can produce a significant united front. But on eschatology we must surely be the laughing stock of unbelievers, at least those who read what we write on the subject. There is, I believe, a fundamental methodological problem here we have not confronted."[33]

Dwight Wilson, professor of history at Bethany Bible College, probably has summed up best the plight of most evangelicals: "The premillenarians' history . . . is strewn with a mass of erroneous speculations which have undermined their credibility. . . . The premillenarians' credibility is at a low ebb because they succumbed to the temptation to exploit every conceivably possible prophetic fulfillment for the sake of their prime objective: evangelism. The doomsaying cry of 'Armageddon Now!' was an effective evangelistic tool of terror to scare people into making decisions for Christ and to stimulate believers to 'witness for Christ' to add stars to their heavenly crowns before it was everlastingly too late. Voices of moderation were less likely to find mass appeal. . . . The success of such evangelistic approaches was to the premillenarians well worth the risk of false identifications in the interpretation of prophecy. . . . The premillenarians see evangelism as the means to save the world and will continue to use this means as a justification to misuse the end."[34]

The reason why Seventh-day Adventists are not caught in the credibility gap that all premillennialists emphasizing an imminent return of Jesus have inevitably found themselves in for generations is simply this: Adventists employ a consistent system of biblical interpretation (hermeneutics) that includes the biblical principle of conditional prophecy. By means of this biblical insight the Bible student will avoid the mistakes and non sequiturs of other, equally sincere, Bible students.

THE END: THE UNIQUE VOICE OF ADVENTISTS

This principle of conditionality is the theme of our next chapter.

References

1. Apocalyptic writings flourished between 200 B.C. and A.D. 150; subject matter focused on the future rather than the present, was chiefly concerned with how God would ultimately conquer the forces of evil, and largely presented through literary imagery such as symbols, numbers, and symmetrical patterns.
2. C. H. Dodd, *The Parables of the Kingdom* (London: Nisbet & Co., Ltd., 1948), pp. 49-51, 203.
3. "The so-called 'second' Coming (not in fact a New Testament phrase) is viewed as the return of the risen Christ in the power of the Spirit. . . . The Second Coming has happened in the return of Christ in the Spirit; the Resurrection of the Body has occurred in the putting on of the new man in the Body of Christ; the Millennium has been inaugurated in the reign of Christ in his Church on earth; the Antichrist is a present reality wherever final refusal meets the Christian preaching; the Messianic Banquet is celebrated whenever the wine is drunk new in the kingdom of God; Satan falls from heaven as each man decides for the Gospel, and in the finished work of Christ the Prince of this world has been judged; the Last Judgment is being wrought out in every moment of choice and decision; Christ is all in all, since all things *have been* reconciled in him." James A. T. Robinson, *In The End, God* (New York: Harper & Row, Publishers, 1968), pp. 71, 77. See also Robinson, *Jesus and His Coming* (New York: Abingdon Press, 1957).
4. Albert Schweitzer, *The Quest of the Historical Jesus* (New York: The Macmillan Company, 1961), p. 360.
5. "According to the New Testament the decisive significance of Jesus Christ is that he—in his person, his coming, his passion, and his glorification—is the eschatological event. . . . We must, therefore, say that to live in faith is to live an eschatological existence, to live beyond the world, to have passed from death to life (cf. John 5:24; 1 John 3:14). Certainly the eschatological existence is already realized in anticipation, for "we walk by faith, not by sight" (2 Corinthians 5:7). This means that the eschatological existence of the believer is not a worldly phenomenon, but is realized in the new self-understanding." Rudolf Bultmann, *Jesus Christ and Mythology* (New York: Charles Scribner's Sons, 1958), pp. 80, 81.
6. Rudolf Bultmann, *"New Testament and Mythology,"* in *Kerygma and Myth*, ed. by Hans Bartsch (New York: Harper & Row, Publishers, Torchbook Series), p. 5.
7. Jurgen Moltmann, *The Theology of Hope* (London: SCM Press, 1967); see also "Theology as Eschatology." *The Future of Hope: Theology as Eschatology*, edited by Frederick Herzog (New York: Herder and Herder, 1970).

CONFLICTING DOCTRINES OF THE SECOND ADVENT

8. Carl E. Braaten, *The Future of God* (New York: Harper & Row, Publishers, 1969), p. 166.
9. John Warwick Montgomery, "Episcopal Futurity and Futility," *Christianity Today*, March 16, 1973, pp. 49, 50.
10. *Ibid.*
11. Adam Clarke, *Clarke's Commentary* (New York: The Methodist Book Concern. n.d.), p. 1054.
12. James White, *Bible Adventism* (Reprint. Nashville Tenn.: Southern Publishing Association, 1972).
13. While writing this chapter (February 1979) the author attended the Earl Lectures at the Pacific School of Religion, Berkeley, California. Imagine his surprise when the program for morning worship included the following words for the closing hymn, "When We All Shall Walk Together" (Tune: "When the Roll Is Called Up Yonder").

> 1. When the trumpet of the Lord shall sound,
>   and guns shall be no more;
>   When the paths of peace are open far and wide,
>   And when all shall cease their fighting
>   And shall build a peaceful world,
>   Then the love of Christ shall rule in every heart.
>
> Refrain: When we all shall walk together,
>   When we all shall walk together,
>   When we all shall walk together,
>   Then the love of Christ shall rule in every heart.
>
> 2. When the rich and poor shall share the blessings
>   of this world of ours,
>   And our God shall wipe away our hates and fears:
>   When the black and brown and white shall walk
>   As friends upon this earth,
>   Then the love of Christ shall rule in every heart.
>
> Refrain
>
> 3. For the beauty all about us here
>   our minds are full of thanks;
>   For pure water and clear air we breathe a prayer;
>   When we use them and we save them
>   For the children yet to come,
>   Then this earth shall be a joy forevermore.

14. Loraine Boettner, *The Millennium* (Philadelphia Presbyterian and Reformed Publishing Company, 1957). See *Christianity Today*, November 3, 1978.
15. J. Marcellus Kik, *An Eschatology of Victory* (Nutley, N.J.: Presbyterian and Reformed Publishing Company, 1971).
16. An excellent help in understanding the error in the "secret rapture"

theory is Ralph Blodgett, *Rapture! Is It for Real?* (Mountain View, California: Pacific Press Publishing Association, 1975).

17. A partial list would include Biola College, Talbot Theological Seminary, Western Conservative Baptist Seminary, Dallas Theological Seminary, and Moody Bible Institute.

18. George Ladd, *The Blessed Hope* (Grand Rapids: Eerdmans, 1956), p. 89.

19. J. Barton Payne, *The Imminent Appearing of Christ* (Grand Rapids: Eerdmans, 1962), p. 39.

20. Hal Lindsey, *The Late Great Planet Earth* (New York: Bantam Books, 1973).

21. For reviews of the historical development of the secret-rapture theory see Millard J. Erickson, *Contemporary Options in Eschatology* (Grand Rapids: Baker Book House, 1977), pp. 111-115; Dave MacPherson, *The Unbelievable Pre-Trib Origin* (Kansas City, Mo.: Heart of America Bible Society, 1973).

22. For a fuller analysis of the dispensationalist-secret rapture error see Erickson, pp. 110-124; George E. Ladd, *Crucial Questions About the Kingdom of God* (Grand Rapids: William B. Eerdmans Publishing Co., 1952), pp. 48-52; C. Vanderwaal, *Hal Lindsey and Biblical Prophecy* (St. Catharines, Ontario: Paideia Press, 1978), pp. 18-45; T. Boersma, *Is the Bible a Jigsaw Puzzle . . .* (St. Catharines, Ontario: Paideia Press, 1978), pp. 1-193.

23. See comments on Daniel 9:24-27 and "The History of the Interpretation of Daniel," pp. 39-78, in *S.D.A. Bible Commentary,* vol. 4, for a fuller discussion.

24. Lindsey, pp. 32-40.

25. J. Barton Payne, "Jesus Is Coming Again: Posttribulation," *Christian Life,* May 1974, and Erickson, pp. 173-181. Dr. Payne has written extensively on last-day prophecy, opposing both pretrib and posttrib positions while maintaining his premillennialist stance. His clearest statement is *The Imminent Appearing of Jesus Christ* (Grand Rapids: William B. Eerdmans Publishing Co., 1962). See also *Encyclopedia of Biblical Prophecy* (New York: Harper & Row).

26. John F. Walvoord, *The Rapture Question* (Findley, Ohio: Dunham Publishing Company, 1957), pp. 16-19.

27. *Ibid.,* p. 19.

28. *Ibid.,* pp. 16, 17.

29. For a valuable review of Israel's place in history and prophecy see Orley M. Berg, *The Restless Land* (Washington, D.C.: Review and Herald Publishing Association, 1974).

30. Ellen G. White, *Review and Herald,* March 22, 1892.

31. Wilbur Smith, "Signs of the Second Advent of Christ," ed. Carl F. H. Henry, *Prophecy in the Making* (Carol Stream, Ill.: Creation House, 1971), pp. 187-213.

32. *Ibid.*

CONFLICTING DOCTRINES OF THE SECOND ADVENT

33. *Christianity Today,* April 13, 1973.

Peter Beyerhaus likewise cautioned fellow evangelicals: "A central concern of evangelical theology should be to establish a common basis of eschatological teaching that is both faithful to the clear texts of biblical prophecies and relevant to events of world history that clearly have an apocalyptic significance. . . .

"This is a most responsible task, as the life and death of Christ's flock is at stake. Therefore it can only be tackled in a highly responsible way. Haphazard hypothesis and speculation must be excluded as much as eccentric exegesis. We must be humble enough to listen to the expository answers of our spiritual fathers and to place our own solution under the correcting judgment of our brethren. Nowhere has evangelical individualism created so many unwarranted doctrinal factions as in eschatology." *Christianity Today,* February 16, 1973.

34. Dwight Wilson, *Armageddon Now!* (Grand Rapids: Baker Book House, 1977), pp. 216-218.

The Principle of Conditional Prophecy

The principle of conditionality is not a hermeneutical gimmick contrived by Seventh-day Adventists to explain the delay in the advent. Conditional prophecy, or controlled uncertainty, is a biblical principle applied to statements of a predictive nature that concern or involve the response of men and women. Whenever an unfolding of events depends upon human choice, certain aspects of prophetic fulfillment are necessarily conditional.

Besides being a hermeneutical principle (examples of which follow) this concept faithfully reflects the character of God. It tells us much about His way of dealing with mankind. He forces no one to do things His way; He waits for His people to "catch on." He is very patient and longsuffering; but eventually what He promises does materialize. What He says *will* be done, eventually *gets* done. However, He often must wait until what He has purposed is accomplished by men and women who have freedom of choice—for that is what the cosmic controversy is all about.[1]

Moses made the principle of conditionality clear in Deuteronomy 28: "And if you obey the voice of the Lord your God, being careful to do all his commandments which I command you this day, the Lord your God will set you high above all the nations of the earth. . . . But if you will not obey the voice of the Lord your God or be careful to do all his commandments and his statutes which I command you this day, then all these curses shall come upon you and overtake you." Verses 1 and 15.

The unnamed prophet emphasized this principle to aging Eli: "Therefore the Lord the God of Israel declares: 'I promised that your house and the house of your father should go in and out before me for ever'; but now the Lord declares: 'Far be it from me; for those who honor me I will honor, and those

THE PRINCIPLE OF CONDITIONAL PROPHECY

who despise me shall be lightly esteemed. Behold, the days are coming, when I will cut off your strength and the strength of your father's house, so that there will not be an old man in your house'." 1 Samuel 2:30, 31.

Jonah had to learn this lesson of conditionality the hard way: "When God saw what they did, how they turned from their evil way, God repented of the evil which he had said he would do to them; and he did not do it. But it displeased Jonah exceedingly, and he was angry." Jonah 3:10-4:1.

Josiah, the young king of Judah, led his people in a remarkable reformation; during his reign idolatry was generally uprooted, the temple service reopened (2 Chronicles 34). The Lord sent the promise: "Because your heart was penitent and you humbled yourself before God when you heard his words against this place and its inhabitants . . . I also have heard you. . . . Behold, I will gather you to your fathers, and you shall be gathered to your grave in peace." 2 Chronicles 34:27, 28.

PROMISES TO JOSIAH WERE CONDITIONAL

But Josiah died in battle, in an act contrary to the will of God. Why? Because he did not obey the warnings given him. The Lord did not give him orders to war against the armies of Egypt. In fact, the Lord gave express orders for Necho, the king of Egypt, to engage in battle the imperialistic western thrusts of Babylon.

Even more interesting, Necho sent special word to Josiah, disclaiming any intention to do Judah harm, emphasizing that Josiah's God was directing Egypt in battle against Babylon: "Cease opposing God, who is with me, lest he destroy you." 2 Chronicles 35:21.

Prudent and wise it would have been for Josiah to accept this message from God. But Josiah disguised himself and led his army into a battle that he never should have joined. In the Battle of Charchemish, Josiah was killed. A man who had been so richly honored by God came to his end, not heeding his God's command.

God's promise that Josiah would die a peaceful death was conditional upon continued obedience. When even the best

THE END: THE UNIQUE VOICE OF ADVENTISTS

go against the word of God, choosing to follow personal inclination, "God could not shield him from the consequences of his act."[2]

Jeremiah conveyed this conditional principle clearly: "If at any time I declare concerning a nation or a kingdom, that I will pluck up and break down and destroy it, and if that nation, concerning which I have spoken, turns from its evil, I will repent of the evil that I intended to do to it. And if at any time I declare concerning a nation or a kingdom that I will build and plant it, and if it does evil in my sight, not listening to my voice, then I will repent of the good which I had intended to do to it." Chapter 18:7-10.

The principle of conditional prophecy, simply stated, recognizes that "the promises and threatenings of God are alike conditional."[3]

ISRAEL, A STRIKING ILLUSTRATION

In our last chapter we noted that the many voices proclaiming our Lord's soon return do so for reasons that Seventh-day Adventists cannot support. One of the chief signs to almost everyone now proclaiming an imminent return of Jesus is the establishment of the state of Israel, in 1948. For Seventh-day Adventists, the political state of Israel has no connection with last-day prophecies.

Chief among the reasons why the state of Israel has no prophetic significance is that after the Jews rejected Jesus as the Messiah God gave to the Christian church the special privileges, responsibilities, and prerogatives once assigned to the ancient Jews. No longer were the Jews to be His special people with a prophetic destiny.

This simple biblical fact has been overlooked or rejected by advocates of the secret-rapture theory and by others who see special prophetic significance in the rise of modern Israel because they ignore the biblical principle of conditional prophecy. Ignoring this hermeneutical principle of biblical exegesis opens the door to a distorted picture of biblical predictions and fulfillments.

Because the experience of Israel is a striking illustration of this biblical principle of conditionality, we should examine

THE PRINCIPLE OF CONDITIONAL PROPHECY

further how this principle has been reflected in Israel's history.

The glory that *could have been* Israel's is probably the saddest story in literature. Placed at the crossroads of the ancient world, "God furnished them with every facility for becoming the greatest nation on the earth."[4]

Israel was to be rewarded with every physical and spiritual blessing as they put into practice the clear-cut principles that God had graciously taught them through His prophets.[5]

The Old Testament records the sad story of how the vineyard of Israel produced, not the mature fruit of Christlike character, but "wild grapes," a misinterpretation and perversion of what the God of Israel was really like. "What more was there to do for my vineyard, that I have not done in it? When I looked for it to yield grapes, why did it yield wild grapes?" Isaiah 5:4.

Even when the Jewish nation was suffering the bitter consequences of disobedience during the Babylonian captivity, God mercifully promised that a restored Israel was possible and that time still remained to recover her special role as His distinguished representative on earth—if the nation would honor His law and submit to His principles. Even then, the Jews could have become, if faithful, the head and not the tail in matters physical and spiritual; all nations would have looked upon Jerusalem as not only the center of wisdom but also the spiritual capital of the world.

But the Jewish nation failed during its second chance. The promises given to Abraham and expanded through the writings of Moses "should have met fulfillment in large measure during the centuries following the return of the Israelites from the lands of their captivity. It was God's design that the whole earth be prepared for the first advent of Christ, even as today the way is preparing for His second coming. At the end of the years of humiliating exile, God graciously gave to His people Israel, through Zechariah, the assurance 'I am returned unto Zion, and will dwell in the midst of Jerusalem: and Jerusalem shall be called a city of truth; and the mountain of the Lord of hosts the holy mountain.' "[6]

The prophecies of the Old Testament that picture Israel

dwelling in peace and prosperity, with all nations beating a path to her doors, could have been fulfilled centuries ago if the Israelites had indeed prepared the world for the first coming of Jesus. But instead of fulfilling their greatest assignment, they missed their last hour of opportunity, and Jesus, their Lord, finally had to pronounce with irrevocable judgment: " 'O Jerusalem, Jerusalem, killing the prophets and stoning those who are sent to you! How often would I have gathered your children together as a hen gathers her brood under her wings, and you would not! Behold, your house is forsaken and desolate.' " Matthew 23:37, 38.

The mistake currently being made regarding the establishment of the modern state of Israel, as a fulfillment of last-day prophecies, is that these prophecies that look forward to a restored Jewish state in the land of Palestine were made either prior to the release of the Jews from their Babylonian captivity, or during the rebuilding days soon after their return. God would have fulfilled these promises if Israel had been faithful and obedient to the conditions stated.

Although God promised a second chance to Israel after their failure leading up to the Babylonian captivity, He promised no third chance to them after they rejected the apostolic message of the first century, which proclaimed the story of the Lord Himself who "came to his own home, and his own people received him not." John 1:11.

But God did not give up, though Israel as a nation failed Him. Although corporate Israel no longer was to function as God's special agent, the Jews who received and obeyed His Son would constitute the new organization through which He would now work.

TRANSITION FROM JEWISH NATION TO CHRISTIAN CHURCH

Paul describes this remarkable transition in Romans 9 to 11, where he appeals to individual Jews (such as himself) to respond to God through Jesus, and join the Gentiles who have found in Him the solution to their anxious, sinful hearts.

Paul makes it very clear that the literal Jew has a future, a

THE PRINCIPLE OF CONDITIONAL PROPHECY

part in the eternal plans of God, but only as a member of the Christian church. Even as individual Gentiles are grafted into the saving fellowship of God's people, so individual Jews would be "grafted back into their own olive tree." Romans 11:24.

In New Testament language, the "Jew" is no longer the literal descendant of Abraham but any person (Hebrew or Gentile) converted to Christ and committed to be His disciple. "For he is not a real Jew who is one outwardly, nor is true circumcision something external and physical. He is a Jew who is one inwardly, and real circumcision is a matter of the heart, spiritual and not literal." Romans 2:28, 29. Indeed, before Jesus returns we expect a large number of our Jewish friends to join those who wait eagerly for Him.[7]

In conclusion, the Old Testament prophecies that depicted a central role for the nation of Israel as (1) God's evangelistic agency for the whole world and (2) the world's center of material and spiritual prosperity have not been fulfilled and will not be fulfilled because Israel as a nation defaulted on her responsibilities. The prophecies of blessings were dependent upon Israel's obedience. The glorious pictures of Zechariah 9 to 14, for example, will not be fulfilled as they could have been.

But the overall drama will be fulfilled. God's plan for the renovation of this earth will be consummated. Sin will be forever obliterated from the universe. But before that happy day a struggle will be waged for the hearts of men on this earth. That struggle will mount in intensity until men everywhere will actually divide themselves over the same issues that Israel as a nation stumbled over centuries ago. To make the nature of this struggle clearer, and to reveal what the church will finally do about it, will be the subject of following chapters in this book.

The hermeneutical principle of conditional prophecy spares the biblical student from misunderstanding the role of modern Israel in the fulfillment of last-day prophecies. This conditionality concept prevents Seventh-day Adventists from falling into the credibility gap afflicting all other premillennialists confronted by their built-in dilemma, namely:

THE END: THE UNIQUE VOICE OF ADVENTISTS

Why hasn't the Lord come when each generation seems to come up with convincing evidence that all the prophetical signs have been fulfilled in their day?

In surveying the various positions of many earnest students of the advent, it seems that only Seventh-day Adventists know why the advent has been delayed and what alone can hasten our Lord's return. On one hand, they know where, and where not, to look for those specific signs that the advent is near. For example, by accepting the biblical principle of conditional prophecy, Adventists are not decoyed into measuring the tempo of last-day events by what happens in the recently established nation of Israel. And there are other examples of where not to look, even though sensational elements and fear-inducing excitement may get temporary attention.

On the other hand, they will recognize the question of great importance before the Christian world in general and Seventh-day Adventists in particular—namely, *what are those conditions* that must be fulfilled in order that Jesus may return in our day?

In our next chapter, we will examine another hermeneutical tool by which we get a clearer picture as to what is on God's mind regarding the future and the end of this world.

References

1. Ellen G. White, *Patriarchs and Prophets* (Mountain View, Calif.: Pacific Press Publishing Association, 1958), pp. 49, 331, 332.
2. White Comments, *S.D.A. Bible Commentary* (Washington, D.C.: Review and Herald Publishing Association, 1957), vol. 2, p. 1039.
3. White, *Selected Messages* (Washington, D.C.: Review and Herald Publishing Association, 1958), bk. 1, p. 67.
4. White, *Christ's Object Lessons*, p. 288.
5. For further study of Israel's projected role as God's Exhibit A demonstration of His principles in Old Testament times and how they failed to fulfill their opportunities, see *S.D.A. Bible Commentary*, vol. 4, pp. 25-38.
6. Ellen G. White, *Prophets and Kings* (Washington, D.C.: Review and Herald Publishing Association, 1917), pp. 703, 704.
7. White, *Evangelism* (Washington, D.C.: Review and Herald Publishing Association, 1946), pp. 578, 579.

The Harvest Principle

The biblical correlate to the concept of conditional prophecy is the harvest principle. That is, God will wait for the maturing of Christian character in a significant number of people as the chief condition determining those events which affect the time when probation for the world will close, and thus the time of the advent.

Other prophetic lines will also converge in the "last days" giving assurance to those who are "awake" and "sober" (1 Thessalonians 5:6) that "the day of the Lord" is at hand. In the following pages, we shall discuss several prophetic conditions that highlight "the last days." These last-day "signs of the times" provide the political and social backdrop for the harvest principle. All biblical descriptions of the last days and events that must "come to pass" may be integrated and subsumed under the harvest principle. Herein lies the secret to the unforced coherence and integrity of Adventist eschatology (the study of the last-day events).

In Mark 4, Jesus explains the nature of the kingdom of God: " 'The kingdom of God is as if a man should scatter seed upon the ground, and should sleep and rise night and day, and the seed should sprout and grow, he knows not how. The earth produces of itself, first the blade, then the ear, then the full grain in the ear. But when the grain is ripe, at once he puts in the sickle, because the harvest has come.' " Verses 26-29.

When Jesus was describing to John on Patmos the nature and timing of His second advent, He reemphasized the harvest principle as the key to an understanding of why all Heaven waits for a delayed harvest down in the twentieth century: "Then I looked, and lo, a white cloud, and seated on the cloud one like a son of man, with a golden crown on his head, and a sharp sickle in his hand. And another angel came

THE END: THE UNIQUE VOICE OF ADVENTISTS

out of the temple, calling with a loud voice to him who sat upon the cloud, 'Put in your sickle, and reap, for the hour to reap has come, for the harvest of the earth is fully ripe.' So he who sat upon the cloud swung his sickle on the earth, and the earth was reaped.'' Revelation 14:14-16.

OUR LORD'S HARVEST ANALOGY

Here, in His masterful way, our Lord compared His second coming to an earthly harvest. In these two texts the Master Teacher is telling us that the goals of the kingdom of God and the field of grain are the same: Neither is ready to harvest unless the seed has matured. When we plant our gardens we do so with the reasonable hope that eventually we will have a harvest. Who plants corn merely to watch it struggle with the weeds? The full-time farmer and the backyard gardener both look toward the ripe harvest as the goal of their labors. No other goal makes sense.

But does a wise gardener determine the time to pick his corn by merely looking at his calendar, checking off the prescribed number of growing days indicated by his seed catalog for that particular seed? Some corn can be ready in 68 days, some in 77 days, late corn in 88 days, he is told. Does he automatically get his kettle boiling, march out to the field, and pick his corn because the calendar says that it is the sixty-eighth day since he planted his early corn?

The seed catalog is not wrong in predicting that there could and should be a harvest of early corn by the sixty-eighth day after planting. The catalog tells the gardener when the harvest should be mature, when it could be picked—if all growing conditions were favorable. But if the summer is too hot or too cold, too dry or too wet, or if the ground is undernourished, the time of the harvest will be directly affected. The gardener must wait until his harvest is ripe, sometimes at a much later period than he had first hoped, because of many growing conditions often beyond his control.

All that we understand about our gardens will help us when we try to understand why Jesus seems to wait, why His return to this earth appears to have been so long delayed. Perhaps Jesus chose to compare the end of this world to a farmer's harvest, because He knew that men and women everywhere understood, to some degree, the hopes and problems connected with harvesting a field of wheat or backyard tomatoes.

WISE FARMERS WAIT

The first lesson we learn from the Lord's analogy is that even as the wise farmer must wait for his seed to mature, so Jesus chooses to wait until the gospel seed has produced a sizable group of mature Christians in the last generation.[1]

Ellen G. White develops the implications of the harvest principle in numerous places, but probably never clearer than in *Christ's Object Lessons:*

"The object of the husbandman in the sowing of the seed and the culture of the growing plant is the production of grain.... So the divine Husbandman looks for a harvest as the reward of His labor and sacrifice. Christ is seeking to reproduce Himself in the hearts of men; and He does this through those who believe in Him. The object of the Christian life is fruit bearing—the reproduction of Christ's character in the believer, that it may be reproduced in others....

" 'When the fruit is brought forth, immediately he putteth in the sickle, because the harvest is come.' Christ is waiting with longing desire for the manifestation of Himself in His church. When the character of Christ shall be perfectly reproduced in His people, then He will come to claim them as His own. It is the privilege of every Christian not only to look for but to hasten the coming of our Lord Jesus Christ (2 Peter 3:12, margin). Were all who profess His name bearing fruit to His glory, how quickly the whole world would be sown with the seed of the gospel. Quickly the last great harvest would be ripened, and Christ would come to gather the precious grain."[2]

Bible writers and Ellen White suggest other interesting parallels between the harvest of the gospel and that of literal seed. Farmers and prophets have several things in common, the chief of which is that both engage in conditional prophecies. Farmers know that they must keep their eyes on their corn rather than on the seed catalog and the calendar.

THE END: THE UNIQUE VOICE OF ADVENTISTS

The wise housewife or farmer knows when the time of the harvest has come on the basis of the predictions in the catalog. But they also know that they must check that green tomato, that unfilled cob of corn, that swelling head of wheat—before they decide to harvest their crop. No one harvests a premature crop. A premature crop is a waste; such harvesting just isn't done. The wise farmer waits for his harvest, for that is what being a farmer is all about.

THE ADVENT DELAYED

Similarly, our Lord is saying to His church that the delay in the harvest of this world has not been due to a change of mind on the part of the divine Husbandman, or because of a mistake in the divine catalog describing the harvest of this world. As far as God is concerned, the harvest could have, and should have, ripened decades ago. The divine catalog said: "Anytime within the generation living in 1844!" We live now in the time of the delayed harvest. The fruit—the Christian witness that reproduces the character of Jesus—has not yet matured as God has wished. Thus, the purpose of planting the gospel seed has not been achieved.

This line of thought is not new to Seventh-day Adventists. In 1883 Ellen White pleaded with fellow church members to understand why Jesus was delaying His return:

"It is true that time has continued longer than we expected in the early days of this message. Our Saviour did not appear as soon as we hoped. But has the word of the Lord failed? Never! It should be remembered that the promises and threatenings of God are alike conditional. . . .

"Had Adventists, after the great disappointment in 1844, held fast their faith, and followed on unitedly in the opening providence of God, receiving the message of the third angel and in the power of the Holy Spirit proclaiming it to the world, they would have seen the salvation of God, the Lord would have wrought mightily with their efforts, the work would have been completed, and Christ would have come ere this to receive His people to their reward."[3]

Unequivocally, as clearly as words can convey thought, Ellen White declared the sad yet challenging truth that the

THE HARVEST PRINCIPLE

return of Jesus was already delayed in the 1880s, that He would continue to wait until His glory, His character, had been reflected in the lives of His followers.[4]

Furthermore, Ellen White warned that Adventists must not, no matter how plausible the reasoning, blame God for the delay in the advent:

"It was not the will of God that the coming of Christ should be thus delayed. God did not design that His people, Israel, should wander forty years in the wilderness. . . . For forty years did unbelief, murmuring, and rebellion shut out ancient Israel from the land of Canaan. The same sins have delayed the entrance of modern Israel into the heavenly Canaan. In neither case were the promises of God at fault. It is the unbelief, the worldliness, unconsecration, and strife among the Lord's professed people that have kept us in this world of sin and sorrow so many years."[5]

In 1901 she counseled, referring to the delayed advent, that "we may have to remain here in this world because of insubordination many more years . . . but for Christ's sake, His people should not add sin to sin by charging God with the consequences of their own wrong course of action."[6]

CHARGING GOD FOR MAN'S FAILURE

How would Seventh-day Adventists charge God with the consequences of "their own wrong course of action"? Surely not directly. Yet, could it be possible, that by forgetting the harvest principle, certain reasons have been advanced that indeed transfer the responsibility for the delay from God's professed people to God Himself!

For example, explanations such as the following tend to transfer the responsibility for the delay from the church on earth to God above: (a) The angels have been judging the dead and the living since 1844, turning each person's page inexorably, tirelessly, day and night, and as soon as the last page is turned, probation will close and the plagues will fall. (b) God has His own celestial clock for all the world's events, the hands move relentlessly, and when the hand strikes midnight, probation will close, regardless of the state of His remnant. (c) The magnitude of reaching the world's billions staggers any reasonable person; whatever nearly three million Adventists do would hardly be noticed; if Jesus is to return, God will have to step in arbitrarily and cut the work short in righteousness. (d) Probation can't close until Turkey comes to her end with none to help her and such a development is not imminent.[7]

But if Jesus could have come long before 1883, as Ellen White often notes,[8] none of these human explanations has validity. The reason for the delay in the advent is contained in the harvest principle. Even though Jesus could have come a century ago, even though the harvest should have ripened four or five generations ago, Jesus will return only when the harvest is ripe. The corollary is simply that world conditions were as ready 100 years ago as they are today; as far as world conditions were concerned, practically all the prophecies regarding the end times had been fulfilled. In 1900, we were told: "This message [of the second coming] is given to men today, and at this time there is coupled with it the announcement of Christ's second coming as at hand. The signs which He Himself gave of His coming have been fulfilled, and by the teaching of God's word we may know that the Lord is at the door."[9]

No prophecy concerning world conditions remained unfulfilled a century ago, except those that describe events that will take place after God decides His people are ready for these events to take place, such as the latter rain, loud cry, shaking time experiences, and those events which are reactions in the secular world to the unprecedented thrust of the church into the public arena.

GOD'S SOVEREIGNTY NOT LIMITED

The harvest principle in no way limits God's sovereignty. Much to the contrary, it only adds to His majesty as One who is patient, merciful, and forbearing for the sake of His universe. The delay only confirms further the nature of the great controversy. God doesn't need anything proven to Him. But He is concerned that the principles of both His government and that of His adversary should develop fully so that there would never be a doubt in any created being's mind ever

THE HARVEST PRINCIPLE

again as to whether God's way is just and merciful. Never again the question whether God could be trusted.[10]

To make clear the eternal differences between God's government of love and law and that of selfish, arrogant greed and force is the central point in the cosmic controversy. The Christian witness in the last generation has a very integral role to play in the final display of God's case. In many ways this awesome responsibility resting on last-day Christians has been described. For example:

"Satan is constantly urging men to accept his principles. Thus he seeks to counterwork the work of God. . . . The Lord desires through His people to answer Satan's charges by showing the result of obedience to right principles.

"All the light of the past, all the light which shines in the present and reaches forth into the future, as revealed in the word of God, is for every soul who will receive it. The glory of this light, which is the very glory of the character of Christ, is to be manifested in the individual Christian, in the family, in the church, in the ministry of the world, and in every institution established by God's people."[11]

But that time when the full harvest of these contrasting principles is on full display is not predetermined by an arbitrary celestial clock that forces God to act before His purposes are fulfilled. The well-attested fact that Jesus could have come and would have come during the lifetime of those who preached His nearness in the 1840s is evidence enough that no arbitrary moment or external, secular condition determines when He is to return. In saying this, we should never overlook the fact that His foreknowledge, characteristic of an omniscient God, permits our Lord to "know" when the church will be finally ready to fulfill His purposes.

To be confused about why Jesus delays His return, to consider the timing of the advent to be an arbitrary decision unrelated to the character readiness of God's remnant people, or to be tied primarily to worldly conditions, tends to foster a climate of apathy, bewilderment, and eventual disillusionment—all tragedies of the credibility gap and unwarranted assumptions.

True it is that "there is a limit beyond which the judgments of Jehovah can no longer be delayed."[12] But that limit is reached when "the final test has been brought upon the world, and all who have proved themselves loyal to the divine precepts have received 'the seal of the living God.' . . . The restraint which has been upon the wicked is removed, and Satan has entire control of the finally impenitent. God's long-suffering has ended."[13]

Let us look at several Ellen White statements that emphasize our Lord's speedy action when wickedness exceeds the forbearance of God:

"Time will last a little longer until the inhabitants of the earth have filled up the cup of their iniquity, and then the wrath of God, which has so long slumbered, will awake."[14]

"The cup of iniquity is nearly filled, and the retributive justice of God is about to descend upon the guilty."[15]

"But there are limits even to the forbearance of God, and many are exceeding these boundaries. They have overrun the limits of grace, and therefore God must interfere and vindicate His own honor. . . . With unerring accuracy the Infinite One still keeps an account with all nations. While His mercy is tendered, with calls to repentance, this account will remain open; but when the figures reach a certain amount which God has fixed, the ministry of His wrath commences. The account is closed. Divine patience ceases."[16]

"The wickedness of the inhabitants of the world has almost filled up the measure of their iniquity. This earth has almost reached the place where God will permit the destroyer to work his will upon it."[17]

Such observations raise important questions: How does one "overrun the limits of grace"? Is there not an obvious connection between the preceding terms and events described, such as beginning "the ministry of His wrath," delivering "the retributive justice of God," filling up "the cup of their iniquity," permitting "the destroyer to work his will"? Why does God hold back His judgments and extend time and forbearance? Will Jesus return, even if none of His followers "reflect the image of Jesus fully"[18] as long as there is enough wickedness to justify God's wrath?

Some brief answers would include the principle that a

THE HARVEST PRINCIPLE

person, or a world of persons, approach the limits of grace when they continue forthrightly to reject the appeal of God. They overrun those limits when they no longer heed the call to repent, care no more for the restraining voice of conscience, and reject with every choice the will of God. For them the warm rays of love and grace only harden resistance. For them there is no more mercy, not because God arbitrarily withdraws it, but because they no longer heed it. They have set their life pattern forever in the direction of their own choosing. For them, it can be said, "He that is unjust, let him be unjust still: and he which is filthy, let him be filthy still." Revelation 22:11, K.J.V.

God will withhold His judgments, restrain His "unmingled wrath," check the hand of Satan the destroyer who is anxious to ravage the earth, "till we have sealed the servants of our God in their foreheads." Revelation 7:3, K.J.V. God will not close probation for the world until a significant portion of His remnant vindicates His government, proves that His way of life can be lived on earth, and proclaims a credible witness to all nations. That segment of His last-day remnant church, which finally proves that the faith of Jesus indeed makes commandment keepers, will be sealed with God's approval. "The seal of the living God will be placed upon those only who bear a likeness to Christ in character."[19]

What is the relationship of the sealing to divine judgments and unmingled wrath? "Just as soon as the people of God are sealed in their foreheads—it is not any seal or mark that can be seen, but a settling into the truth, both intellectually and spiritually, so they cannot be moved—just as soon as God's people are sealed and prepared for the shaking, it will come."[20]

Our Lord is very gracious (that is His nature) to forbear with arrogant sinners and listless church members. He knows that His message is not getting a fair hearing when proclaimed by people who do not reflect truth, self-denial, and graciousness in their lives. He knows that many conscientious people long for reality and substance in their religious outreach. He will not close this world's probation until all living at a given time have had a fair opportunity to

THE END: THE UNIQUE VOICE OF ADVENTISTS

see the difference between those who truly keep His commandments and those who do less.

Those who forthrightly reject the life-style described as keeping "the commandments of God and the faith of Jesus" (Revelation 14:12) will get their way: They will be left alone by God. Selfish, grasping, coercive men and women, unrestrained by a conscience that no longer speaks and urged on by Satan, will plunge this world into "one, great, final trouble."[21] God, not men, is keeping the account. He will know when the account is closed, when there is no more to add to the right or to the left in the great harvest ledger.

BRINGING THE WORLD TO DECISION

To bring the world to that moment of decision is the first order of business for the church that truly wants to hasten the advent. Only pure, honest people can bring credibility to God's last message of mercy to this world. God has promised to provide marvelous power on behalf of committed people. When His people are ready to be entrusted with this power, when God can give His power to His people and not be embarrassed by what would be done with it, then "there will be a series of events revealing that God is master of the situation. The truth will be proclaimed in clear, unmistakable language. As a people we must prepare the way of the Lord under the overruling guidance of the Holy Spirit. The gospel is to be given in its purity."[22]

Among the many facts about the end of the world that we can be sure of is this: God will not wait a moment longer than necessary to recognize the fulfillment of His purposes. "Like the stars in the vast circuit of their appointed path, God's purposes know no haste and no delay."[23] When the gospel seed has ripened—one of the primary purposes of the plan of salvation—there will be no delay in giving the order, "Put in your sickle, and reap." Revelation 14:16.

No man or devil can delay God's harvest when the conditions have been fulfilled, when the harvest is "ripe," when His purposes are accomplished. And His purpose for His church is clear:

"The purpose which God seeks to accomplish through His

THE HARVEST PRINCIPLE

people today is the same that He desired to accomplish through Israel. . . . By beholding the goodness, the mercy, the justice, and the love of God revealed in the church, the world is to have a representation of His character. And when the law of God is thus exemplified in the life, even the world will recognize the superiority of those who love and fear and serve God above every other people on the earth. . . . It is His purpose that those who practice His holy precepts shall be a distinguished people."[24]

"It is God's purpose that His people shall be a sanctified, purified holy people, communicating light to all around them. It is His purpose that, by exemplifying the truth in their lives, they shall be a praise in the earth. . . . If those who profess to believe in Christ as their Saviour reach only the low standard of worldly measurement, the church fails to bear the rich harvest that God expects."[25]

There will be a harvest! This world with its miseries will not drag on into an endless future. There will be a people prepared to meet the Lord and who fulfill His long-range purpose. "The great, grand work of bringing out a people who will have Christlike characters, and who will be able to stand in the day of the Lord, is to be accomplished."[26]

A sad part of the harvest principle is that not all that matures will be fruit of good seed. Every harvester sorts out the mature grain from the weeds. Not all tomatoes are to be eaten.

Whether wheat or tares, a harvest there will ultimately be. The universe as well as mankind everywhere on planet Earth will see on an unprecedented scale, the ripening of the gospel seed exhibited in mature Christlike persons living during the stress of the last days. Also on display will be the full-grown products of evil: selfish thoughts and rebel actions exhibited in those persons symbolized by the tares. Matthew 13:24-30.

As time goes on, the Spirit of God will be resisted more and more, His restraining voice ignored, permitting unbridled evil to grow worse. The fallout of unrestrained evil may be thinly covered with the cosmetics of technological wonder and worldly prudence, but the cancerous corruption of even traditional bastions of honor and integrity will mark

THE END: THE UNIQUE VOICE OF ADVENTISTS

a new and bleak day for many countries.[27]

A direct correlation seems to exist between the ripening index of God's people and a corresponding maturing of selfishness in those developing the characteristics that reflect the image of the archrebel. Jesus did not always arouse the best feelings and action in those He met—even gracious Jesus did not always bring out the best in people. When His character is being reflected more and more, qualitatively and quantitatively, in the time of the harvest, His people can expect predictable responses such as He endured. Revelation 12:17. In fact, the maturing of God's people will evoke previously curious or hesitant people into a mind-set of either acceptance or rejection of those life principles that leave no room for neutrality. The clearer the qualitative distinction of God's people, the sooner will be the worldwide conflict over the specific issues of commandment keeping and personal loyalties.

The harvest principle, as an explanation for the delayed advent, is not something recently thought up. It is not a face-saving device in the twentieth century, as Adventists try to avoid embarrassment when they explain why they have been proclaiming the nearness of the advent since 1844. Adventist writers in the mid-nineteenth century understood well the implication of the harvest principle and the delayed advent. P. Gerard Damsteegt has given us a very helpful guide to early Adventist thought, a truly rigorous examination of key Adventist concepts, in his *Foundations of the Seventh-day Adventist Message and Mission.*[28]

Dr. Damsteegt noted that Ellen and James White, in independent publications, spoke forcefully regarding the delayed advent as early as 1856.[29]

He noted that various Adventist leaders, including Loughborough, Bourdeau, Matteson, J. H. Waggoner, and Uriah Smith, joined with the Whites in connecting character preparation, or lack of it, with the return of Jesus.[30]

Various Adventist leaders are quoted, including James White, Uriah Smith, and Ellen White, emphasizing the responsibility of church members for delaying the promised work of the Holy Spirit—emphasizing, for example, that

THE HARVEST PRINCIPLE

God was "waiting for his people to get right . . . before he adds many more to our numbers."[31]

Damsteegt observed that the Laodicean motif, directed to Seventh-day Adventists by Seventh-day Adventists "provided a rationale for the delay of the parousia."[32]

As we have noted, the harvest principle is a biblical concept. Jesus employed this principle when He answered His disciples' questions, "What shall be the sign of thy coming, and of the end of the world?" Matthew 24:3, K.J.V.

Before giving His answer, which is not complete without the three parables in Matthew 25, Jesus laid down an oft-overlooked caution: "Take heed that no one leads you astray." Matthew 24:4. These few words have been probably the counsel most overlooked by those concerned about the second advent through the centuries.[33] But in what specific areas, with what misread "signs," would sincere Christians become confused and misled?

He spoke of Jesus-impersonators who will arise in every generation until the close of time—the perennial cults with their charismatic leaders.[34] And then He warned, "You will hear of wars and rumors of wars, . . . famines and earthquakes" [that is, you will think that the worst has come, that civilization is doomed, nothing greater can happen to this old world, that this surely must be Armageddon[35]] but, "see that you are not alarmed." Chapter 24:6, 7.

Jesus was saying, Bartholomew, there will always be famines and earthquakes. Andrew, the unending pendulum of war and peace will swing back and forth for as long as time lasts. Nathanael, Thomas, don't be led astray into thinking these inevitable results of universal sin are special signs that my return is near; they are merely the continuing signs that sinful, greedy men and women will never make a paradise out of this planet. John, this world will never get better, no matter how ingenious man becomes.

Years ago, the longtime *Review* editor, James White, emphasized these points to our church: "Wars, pestilences, famines, and earthquakes are not the surest signs of the end. These have ever existed. We may have war, then peace, pestilence, then health, famine, then plenty, earthquakes,

THE END: THE UNIQUE VOICE OF ADVENTISTS

then the bowels of the earth may be quiet; but the message of the third angel is given but once. The progress of this work in fulfillment of prophecy is the highest and brightest light now shining in the religious heavens. Those looking at the Eastern question will probably be disappointed [those who placed great emphasis on Turkey as the King of the North who would come to her end with none to help her]; but we may bear our whole weight upon the last message without fear of disappointment. As we now see our worldwide message extending to the nations, we see the fulfillment of prophecy, and the clearest sign of the close of the work, and the consummation of the hope of the church."[36]

James White correctly understood our Lord's emphasis in Matthew 24. The key to the return of Jesus depends upon how soon "this gospel of the kingdom will be preached throughout the whole world," for only then will the end come. Verse 14. God is concerned with the whole world and not only with a relatively few fortunate people who have had easy access to the Bible, to Christian parents, or to Seventh-day Adventist pioneers.

The Seventh-day Adventist Church is thus a world-conscious movement, forever compelled to think globally, and to see its mission in global terms. "This gospel of the kingdom" is the good news about how God will save men and women from their sins. The story of how God reaches out to pardon all mankind, how He stands ready to provide the power to keep from sinning, is the best news that any man or woman, regardless of his station in life, can ever hear.

But to be believable, this gospel must be validated in human experience. More than being merely told, it must be lived. Only a living demonstration of the "good news"—a people open to others, active and global in their service—will give credible evidence that God's kingdom is real, that what these Christlike men and women say about God's gift of pardon and power has the ring of truth.

Ellen White emphasized often how the "gospel of the kingdom" does its work:

"In order to convince others of the power of Christ's grace, we must know its power in our own hearts and lives.

THE HARVEST PRINCIPLE

The gospel we present for the saving of souls must be the gospel by which our own souls are saved. Only through a living faith in Christ as a personal Saviour is it possible to make our influence felt in a skeptical world. . . . By the power of His grace manifested in the transformation of character the world is to be convinced that God has sent His Son as its Redeemer."[37]

The importance of the harvest principle is heightened when we couple Matthew 24:14 with those words quoted earlier: "*When* the character of Christ shall be perfectly reproduced in His people, *then* He will come to claim them as His own."[38]

Jesus was trying to give all adventists through the centuries a precautionary message with this early warning in Matthew 24. James White and others heard Him plainly. Many did not. Jesus knew how the body chemistry works. He knew that emotions and personal involvement tend to shape the way men think about the problems around them. He knew that those calamities that happened close to home, or in a person's own time, always loom up as the worst or the biggest. The bubonic plague that destroyed a fourth of the population of Europe in the 1300s, those incredible earthquakes in China killing 830,000 in 1556 and 180,000 in 1920, ravaging hordes sweeping over the Roman Empire in A.D. 400 and 500, or Adolf Hitler's armies and Gestapo in 1941, and untold horrors more—all seemed more than mankind could take, especially to those involved. All were enormous evidences that this world is experiencing the consequences of man's sins and Satan's madness.

But Jesus did more than tell us what not to look at. In His answer to the disciples' question, Jesus placed His emphasis not on the state of the world but on the state of His followers.

Why did Jesus want us to keep our eyes on what He expects from His church, rather than on the world, when we are looking for clues as to the nearness of the advent? For this reason: To place undue emphasis on world conditions, always in turmoil, as the chief signs of the end of the world, would be similar to a farmer saying, "I oiled my combine, it

THE END: THE UNIQUE VOICE OF ADVENTISTS

must be time to harvest the wheat." Or, "It looks like there will be a bad thunderstorm; it must be time to pick my corn." There is as much relationship between a thunderstorm and picking ripe corn as between distress in the world and the readiness of the church for the advent.

But what Jesus does say about the state of the world at the time of the end is recorded in Matthew 24:37-39: "As were the days of Noah, so will be the coming of the Son of man. For as in those days before the flood they were eating and drinking, marrying and giving in marriage, until the day when Noah entered the ark, and they did not know until the flood came and swept them all away, so will be the coming of the Son of man."

The conditions of the world prior to the close of probation will probably give the last generation no more direct warning to get ready for Christ's coming than the conditions of the world prior to the Flood encouraged Noah's neighbors to join him in the ark.

Our Lord's reference to Noah as an illustration of how this world will be thinking, and what it will be generally experiencing, in those days when probation closes must not be passed by lightly.

Let's think about what the Lord wants to tell us when He compares Noah's generation with history's last generation, which will also experience the shutting of a door of mercy on those who refuse God's gracious invitation.

References

1. The reason why God waits for mature Christians as the fruit of the gospel seed will be discussed in chapter seven.
2. Ellen G. White, *Christ's Object Lessons,* pp. 67, 69.
3. White, *Selected Messages,* bk. 1, pp. 67, 68.

In 1898 Ellen White noted: "By giving the gospel to the world it is in our power to hasten our Lord's return. We are not only to look for but to hasten the coming of the day of God. 2 Peter 3:12, margin. Had the church of Christ done her appointed work as the Lord ordained, the whole world would before this [1898] have been warned, and the Lord Jesus would have come to our earth in power and great glory."—White, *The Desire of Ages,* pp. 633, 634. For an extended list of references wherein Ellen White noted the delay in the advent, see Appendix A.

THE HARVEST PRINCIPLE

  4. "The light of His glory—His character—is to shine forth in His followers. Thus they are to glorify God, to lighten the path to the Bridegroom's home, to the city of God, to the marriage supper of the Lamb.... His character is to be made known. Into the darkness of the world is to be shed the light of His glory, the light of His goodness, mercy, and truth.... The children of God are to manifest His glory. In their own life and character they are to reveal what the grace of God has done for them."—White, *Christ's Object Lessons,* pp. 414-416.
  5. White, *Selected Messages,* bk. 1, pp. 68, 69.
  6. White, *Evangelism,* p. 696.
  7. See Gary Land's excellent historical review of this particular "reason," or "sign," that some have used in past years, in his article, "The Perils of Prophesying," *Adventist Heritage,* vol. 1, no. 1, Jan. 1974, p. 28.
  8. See Appendix A for a list of such references.
  9. White, *Christ's Object Lessons,* p. 227.
  10. White, *Patriarchs and Prophets,* pp. 41-43, 48, 49.
  11. White, *Testimonies,* vol. 6, p. 11. A fuller explanation regarding the importance of this public demonstration of God's principles in the last days and its integral part in the culmination of the great controversy will be found in chapter seven.
  12. White, *Prophets and Kings,* p. 417.
  13. White, *The Great Controversy,* pp. 613, 614.
  14. White, *Testimonies* (Mountain View, Calif.: Pacific Press Publishing Association, 1948), vol. 1, p. 363 (1863).
  15. White, *Testimonies,* vol. 4, p. 489 (1885).
  16. White, *Testimonies,* vol. 5, p. 208 (1889).
  17. White, *Testimonies,* vol. 7, p. 141 (1902).
  18. White, *Early Writings* (Washington, D.C.: Review and Herald Publishing Association, 1882), p. 71.
  19. Ellen G. White Comments on Revelation 7:1-3, *S.D.A. Bible Commentary,* vol. 7, p. 970.
  20. *Ibid.,* Ellen G. White Comments on Ezekiel 9:2-4, vol. 4, p. 1161.
  21. Ellen G. White, *The Great Controversy,* p. 614.
  22. White, *Testimonies,* vol. 9, p. 96.
  23. White, *The Desire of Ages,* p. 32.
  24. White, *Testimonies,* vol. 6, p. 12.
  25. White, *Testimonies,* vol. 8, p. 14. "It is the purpose of God to glorify Himself in His people before the world. He expects those who hear the name of Christ to represent Him in thought, word, and deed.... The life that Christ lived in this world, men and women can live through His power and under His instruction. In their conflict with Satan they may have all the help that He had. They may be more than conquerors through Him who loved them and gave Himself for them.... The truth for this time is to appear in its power in the lives of those who believe it, and is to be imparted to the world. Believers are to represent in their lives its power to sanctify and ennoble."—White, *Testimonies,* vol. 9, pp. 21, 22.

THE END: THE UNIQUE VOICE OF ADVENTISTS

26. Ellen G. White, *Testimonies*, vol. 6, p. 129.
27. See White, *Testimonies*, vol. 5, pp. 451, 525, 712; White, *The Great Controversy*, pp. 581, 590-592 for predictions regarding erosion of constitutional integrity in the United States. Carried out for what seems the best of reasons and for the greater good for the most people, this restriction of previously reverenced constitutional liberties will be most painful for those who prize the founding principles of this "land of the free."
28. P. Gerard Damsteegt, *Foundations of the Seventh-day Adventist Message and Mission* (Grand Rapids: William B. Eerdmans Publishing Company, 1977).
29. *Ibid.*, pp. 217, 219.
30. *Ibid.*, pp. 232-235.
31. *Ibid.*, pp. 244-248.
32. *Ibid.*, p. 248.
33. See Appendix B for a sampling of how serious Christians, through the centuries, by misunderstanding our Lord's warning regarding signs, were convinced that they were living in the "last days."
34. For an extensive review of modern cults, Jesus-impersonators, and other extreme movements and ideologies that function as substitutes for a proper relationship between Jesus and His followers, see Kurt E. Koch, *Satan's Devices*, translated by Michael Freeman (Grand Rapids: Kregel Publications, 1978).
35. See Dwight Wilson, *Armageddon Now!* for an extensive review of premillennialist presentations, especially from 1917 to the present, that have viewed successive crises as signs of the end and impending Armageddon.
36. James White, *Review and Herald*, November 29, 1877.
37. Ellen G. White, *The Ministry of Healing*, pp. 469, 470. "The world will be convinced not so much by what the pulpit teaches as by what the church lives. The preacher announces the theory of the gospel, but the practical piety of the church demonstrates its power."—White, *Testimonies*, vol. 6, p. 260.
38. White, *Christ's Object Lessons*, p. 69. (Italics supplied.)

They Refused "To Know"

Two men were observing two other men, each of whom was carrying a sign. One sign read, "The world is about to end!" The other, "The world will never end!" One of the bystanders said to the other, "One's a pessimist and the other's an optimist. But I am not sure which is which!"

Our modern dilemma! For every expert who decries the pending doom of planet Earth, there is another, equally academically and technologically trained, who argues convincingly that the future never looked brighter!

Does the Christian have any clue as to who's right? No question about it—God doesn't play hide and seek with us. He shares His mind regarding the future.

But what we hear from God is often not what one would expect or even want to hear. It often seems contrary to reason! Imagine, for example, telling a man with a family to build a gigantic boat on dry land—and then to invite all who would listen, none of whom had ever seen rain, to enter this boat and thus escape being drowned in a flood!

God's way of deciding who should be saved or lost is preeminently wise and simple—but so hard for those who want everything proved to their eyes and ears before they say Yes. Such a Yes is always too late, chiefly because they are misunderstanding the point of what goodness and badness is all about.

For instance, Jesus said that the end of the world would be "as were the days of Noah." Matthew 24:37. If this is one of the Lord's clearest clues, what can we learn from Noah's experience?

Noah was known as "a preacher of righteousness." 2 Peter 2:5, K.J.V. That is, he preached a message concerning righteousness. He preached a new life-style, at least a life-style in sharp contrast with his generation. He called on his neigh-

THE END: THE UNIQUE VOICE OF ADVENTISTS

bors to obey their Creator and conform to His likeness. To do contrary would be to allow "every imagination of the thoughts . . . [to be] evil continually." Genesis 6:5. A pattern of life contrary to God's life-style leads to a condition "corrupt in God's sight," and the earth becomes "filled with violence." Genesis 6:11.

At the end of time, again God's message will be emphatically a call to righteousness—an appeal to man to accept God's pardon and power in order to live "blameless in his generation," even as Noah was declared to be in his. Genesis 6:9.

Before the end of time, in the last days preceding judgment, there will be such people who, like Noah, will respond to the call for righteousness—a "call for the endurance of the saints, those who keep the commandments of God and the faith of Jesus." Revelation 14:12. More about this in our next chapter.

But what will world conditions be like during those last days before Jesus returns? One of our clues is: As were the days of Noah." Matthew 24:37. Noah preached his message of righteous living by faith at a time when "the earth was corrupt in God's sight, and . . . filled with violence." Genesis 6:11.

VIOLENT, DECADENT SOCIETY NOT ENOUGH

Fact one: It is interesting to observe that a violent, morally decadent society in Noah's day was not sufficient argument for most people that the end was at hand. Men and women are not frightened for long by the so-called breakdown of society.

Strange but true—fear is not a lasting emotion. It is a highly effective and persuasive technique used by demagogues, shortsighted parents, politicians, and preachers to get immediate results. But impulsive decisions do not last. Nothing is really changed.[1]

Fear is a negative emotion that temporarily stops a particular action; but fear cannot be relied upon to induce a positive change. God, through His prophets in all ages, has presented fearful alternatives as He appealed to people to consider

THEY REFUSED "TO KNOW"

their ways. But, His main emphasis has been the positive appeal, fleshed out with love and grace. For this reason, persuasive techniques that appeal primarily to a fear response, such as appealing to others on the basis of judgments to come, that hellfire awaits them, that the world cannot last another ten years because of its pollution, population, and natural resource problems—all are doomed to fail, if a positive, changed life-style is the result desired.

Although many were moved temporarily by fear, Noah's hearers would not truly repent and live righteous lives by faith in their Creator.[2] Furthermore, God did not want merely fearful people in the ark; He knows that only those committed to keep His commandments and live by faith in His promises of pardon and power are truly safe to save. It is easy to baptize the fearful; it is another matter to build up the church with those who will endure unto the end, committed to His commandments and motivated by the faith of Jesus.

DID NOT KNOW THE TRUTH

Fact two: Noah's generation "did not know." Matthew 24:39. What did they not know? They thought they knew much. They "knew," on the basis of anything that could be seen or heard, that there was no reason to expect doom. True, the world was a mess, society was in constant upheaval and wars were imminent. But what's new? Generations of people can get used to tensions and temporary solutions. For Noah's generation, the future looked bright; after all, the professors, religious leaders, and scientists told them it would be!

Apply fact two to the end of the world: When the door of probation is shut, on the basis of anything that can be seen or heard, this world will look safe enough to last for generations to come—Satan will make sure of that!

Peter, under divine inspiration, reminds us that "scoffers will come in the last days with scoffing, following their own passions and saying, 'Where is the promise of his coming?' " 2 Peter 3:3, 4.

All this suggests that those concerned exclusively with pessimistic predictions, regarding the state of the world be-

THE END: THE UNIQUE VOICE OF ADVENTISTS

fore the close of probation, will be disappointed and probably just as lost as those who scoffed at Noah.

Ellen White joins Peter in noting:

"Come when it may, the day of God will come unawares to the ungodly. When life is going on in its unvarying round; when men are absorbed in pleasure, in business, in traffic, in money-making; when religious leaders are magnifying the world's progress and enlightenment, and the people are lulled in a false security—then, as the midnight thief steals within the unguarded dwelling, so shall sudden destruction come upon the careless and ungodly, 'and they shall not escape.' "[3]

"Christ declares that there will exist similar unbelief concerning His second coming. . . . When the professed people of God are uniting with the world, living as they live, and join with them in forbidden pleasures; when the luxury of the world becomes the luxury of the church; when the marriage bells are chiming, and all are looking forward to many years of worldly prosperity—then, suddenly as the lightning flashes from the heavens, will come the end of their bright visions and delusive hopes."[4]

"The crisis is stealing gradually upon us. The sun shines in the heavens, passing over its usual round, and the heavens still declare the glory of God. Men are still eating and drinking, planting and building, marrying, and giving in marriage. Merchants are still buying and selling. Men are jostling one against another, contending for the highest place. Pleasure lovers are still crowding to theaters, horse races, gambling halls. The highest excitement prevails, yet probation's hour is fast closing, and every case is about to be eternally decided. Satan sees that his time is short. He has set all his agencies at work that men may be deceived, deluded, occupied and entranced, until the day of probation shall be ended, and the door of mercy be forever shut."[5]

In other words, those unprepared for the close of probation will not "know" the truth about transpiring events because they refuse to know. They prefer to "know" what best supports their personal desires and selfish ambitions. They know only what coincides with their presuppositions.

THEY REFUSED "TO KNOW"

Fact three: It seems that world conditions prior to the close of probation will give the last generation no more direct warning than world conditions, prior to the Flood, gave to Noah's hearers.

PARADOX OF HORROR

How can this be? It's the dilemma of the cartoon at the beginning of this chapter—for every pessimist there is an optimist. It's the paradox of horror—to get repeated doses of outrage and horror inoculates one into insensitivity. We learn from biblical clues, and those of Ellen White, that world conditions *prior* to the unprecedented time of trouble (when all the imaginations of science fiction writers will be surpassed by reality) may not seem sufficiently dreadful to cause the world's billions to hasten in repentance.

After living through decades of unprecedented global horror, teetering for years on the brink of nuclear disasters, numb with statistics describing millions living on a starvation level or plagued by pollution disasters—more of the same only seems to anesthetize further the sensibilities of the people. We find ourselves turning the pages of newspapers or magazines, each full of incredible disaster somewhere, as if horror is as normal as the weather report.

In fact, prospects of a peaceful, pleasant world may be more promising and believable for those living just before the close of probation than at any other time in world history. If the world appears on the verge of removing dreaded physical diseases, pollution problems, hunger, and poverty, as well as establishing an unprecedented world peace federation, will not dire warnings of the end of the world seem as unreal and unbelievable as the words of lonely Noah as he implored his neighbors to enter the ark?

The same open disdain, ridicule, and general unconcern given to Noah's message of doom will be duplicated as time runs out in the days immediately before the close of probationary time.[6] As far as observable data are concerned, and with the numbness that comes after a half century cycle of unrelenting tensions and periodic relief, emotionally drained men and women may think of good reasons to discount and

THE END: THE UNIQUE VOICE OF ADVENTISTS

write off the warnings of Seventh-day Adventists.

No question about it—troubles will be rampant and electronically presented before most families on all continents in living color on the 6:00 p.m. news. As time goes on—and with more people—more troubles can be expected on an increasingly greater scale. But mankind has developed an enormous capacity to adjust to such troubles. Furthermore, in spite of it all, men and women seem profoundly eager to believe that technology will forever come up with whatever is necessary to eventually wipe out all such causes for anxiety.

MUCH TO CALM FEAR

In the midst of troubles and tensions, men and women will have much to stimulate their hopes and comfort their fears. Books for both the sophisticated and the common mind, television programs, seminars, and university classrooms—all are reminding us of the giant leaps in solving problems that technology has given the world, especially in the last twenty-five years. Problems that seemed formidable only a quarter century ago are forgotten as if they never existed—or remembered only as relics of long-ago medieval times. Think of what the transistor and microelectronics have done for almost every industry. Or the Salk vaccine, CAT bodyscanners, Teflon, lasers, polymers.

And we, according to many experts, can look forward to food supplies harvested through aquaculture rather than agriculture; weather manipulation and precise prediction; frozen embryos guaranteed from birth defects, and with all characteristics categorized, such as color of hair and eyes, size, IQ, and sex, all ready for the order from prospective parents; genetic therapy whereby appropriate dosages of DNA will remove all tendencies of allergy, obesity, arthritis, and cancer; Cyborgs (people with artificial parts); improved healing via mind control and endorphins; safe, clean inexhaustible laser fusion solving a large percentage of world energy problems; and high strength structural material and super-duty fabrics—and the list is truly endless.[7]

No wonder Ellen White warned that probation will close

THEY REFUSED "TO KNOW"

"when religious leaders are magnifying the world's progress and enlightenment,"[8] when "all are looking forward to many years of worldly prosperity."[9]

No small wonder that Satan will so arrange matters that this world amidst its "normal" tensions and moral decadence, will be "deceived, deluded, occupied, and entranced,"[10] regarding the truth of impending judgment. He will not play into God's hands by permitting society to fall apart drastically or by manipulating the forces of nature so that this planet is a denuded wasteland any more than he did in Noah's day prior to the end of the pre-Flood world. He will deceive, delude, and entrance so that whatever is intrinsically bad about this planet is balanced off with plausible, enthralling prospects of a world emerging from its growing pains.

One of the chief purposes of the Seventh-day Adventist Church is to tell the truth about the future. We believe, going back to the cartoon at the beginning of this chapter, that the Bible makes it clear that the pessimists are wrong—the future is not hopeless. The world will not end in either a whimper or a bang. World nuclear powers will not incinerate the earth; we will not drown or be suffocated in our own garbage, nor shrivel up in mass starvation.

And the Bible makes it clear that optimists are wrong—the future is not in the hands of ingenious men who, up to now, have always come up with the necessary solutions. Technology will not cure, for example, the self-interest of relatives, or neighbors, or nations, as they grab for what they have not earned, trampling others in their reach. Technology may recycle used glass and metals but not the rising tide of moral garbage that mocks the rising standards of living everywhere.

What indeed could be more suffocating than a disease-cured world, filled with homes for all, guaranteeing adequate food for every man, woman, and child (all very probable expectations)—if that world wallows in its comforts and scorns the time-honored values of respect for property rights, fidelity, honesty, purity, and industry?

In summary, Seventh-day Adventists are destined to tell the truth about the future, to proclaim the gospel loud and

THE END: THE UNIQUE VOICE OF ADVENTISTS

clear and say what God has on His mind regarding how this world will come to its end. Its mission is strikingly similar to that of Noah's prior to the Flood. In fact, the kind of world in which Adventists are to proclaim their message is also strikingly similar to Noah's day, as Jesus made clear in Matthew 24:37-39.

Strange as it may seem today, those who died in the Flood thought that their civilization would go on forever. World conditions did not compel Noah's neighbors to listen to him as if they were listening to their last chance. Much to the contrary! Likewise, world conditions, in the last days, will not become so hopeless, so impressively pessimistic, that thoughtful people are compelled to run to the Adventist church for fear of what is about to happen. "As were the days of Noah, so will be the coming of the Son of man."

Perhaps the sliest, most sinister plan Satan has will not be cloaked in the fear engendered by the pessimists but wrapped in the hope and explanations inspired by worldly optimists. The air of optimism finally choked those who laughed at Noah.

But "as were the days of Noah, so will be the coming of the Son of man." Those who are lost, unprepared for the seven last plagues (Revelation 16), religious perhaps but not committed, will be looking for "signs" other than the preaching of righteousness and the invitation of the Spirit to join those who "keep the commandments of God and the faith of Jesus." Revelation 14:12. They "will not know," when the door is shut because they refuse "to know." What a pity!

But what was our Lord's description of the kind of people *who are ready* when the door is shut? He looks at them from at least four different angles in Matthew 24 and 25—the subject of our next chapter.

References

1. Those who appeal to the fear instinct "make an impression upon the people [but] do not work from the right standpoint. The feelings of the people may be stirred and their fears aroused, but they do not move from principle. An excitement is created; but when the time passes, as it has done repeatedly, those who moved out upon time fall back into coldness,

darkness, and sin, and it is almost impossible to arouse their consciences without some great excitement."—White, *Testimonies*, vol. 4, p. 308.
  2. Ellen G. White, *Patriarchs and Prophets*, p. 97.
  3. White, *The Great Controversy*, p. 38. See also Ellen G. White Comments, *S.D.A. Bible Commentary*, vol. 5, p. 1122.
  4. *Ibid.*, p. 338.
  5. Ellen G. White, *The Desire of Ages*, p. 636. See White, *Patriarchs and Prophets*, p. 104.
  6. "In Noah's day the inhabitants of the old world laughed to scorn what they termed the superstitious fears and forebodings of the preacher of righteousness. He was denounced as a visionary character, a fanatic, an alarmist. 'As it was in the days of Noah, so shall it be also in the days of the Son of man.' Men will reject the solemn message of warning in our day, as they did in Noah's time. . . . This is the attitude of the world today. Unbelief is widespread, and the preaching of Christ's coming is mocked at and derided. This makes it all the more essential that those who believe present truth should show their faith by their works. They should be sanctified through the truth which they profess to believe. . . . Abundant time was given them to turn from their sins, overcome their bad habits, and develop righteous characters. But inclination to sin, though weak at first with many, strengthened through repeated indulgence and hurried them on to irretrievable ruin. The merciful warning of God was rejected with sneers, with mockery and derision; and they were left in darkness to follow the course that their sinful hearts had chosen. But their unbelief did not hinder the predicted event."—White, *Testimonies*, vol. 4, p. 308.
  7. See Hiley H. Ward, *Religion 2101 A.D.*, pp. 1-42; Toffler, pp. 185-214, 239-241; Gene Bylinsky, "Shiva: The Next Step to Fusion Power," *Fortune*, January 30, 1978.
  8. Ellen G. White, *Great Controversy*, p. 38.
  9. *Ibid.*, p. 338.
  10. White, *The Desire of Ages*, p. 636.

What Jesus Waits For

Seventh-day Adventists, by definition, are people concerned about the end of time—that is, they are eschatologically oriented. They see in their task a twin purpose: to alert and persuade the world regarding God's last call and to prepare themselves to meet their Lord. They accept the biblical admonition that not all who believe in the second advent will be saved, not all who carry Christ's name reveal His character. See Matthew 7:21-27; 2 Peter 3:11-14.

The chief concern of serious Adventists is to be faithful to the God they represent, to be fit to be used by Him in proclaiming His judgment hour messages to the world; they want to be among that group described in Revelation 14:12—"Here is a call for the endurance of the saints, those who keep the commandments of God and the faith of Jesus."

Jesus pointed to this same concern in Matthew 24: " 'Who then is the faithful and wise servant, whom his master has set over his household, to give them their food at the proper time? Blessed is that servant whom his master when he comes will find so doing.' " Verses 45, 46.

That is the important question today: "Who then is the faithful and wise servant?" In other words, for whom is Jesus waiting in the late twentieth century? Jesus did not leave us to wonder. He proceeded to answer His own question by giving us four picture stories in Matthew 24 and 25, each describing the "faithful and wise" servants who make up that last-day group described in Revelation 14:12. These colorful descriptions characterize the kind of people who will be ready for probationary time to close; they are prepared for Jesus to come, and they are busy helping others to be ready.

The common thread running through our Lord's answer to His question (Matthew 24:45) and ours is that readiness for

WHAT JESUS WAITS FOR

the advent is not a matter of crash preparation, as if one were preparing for an approaching hurricane. Although urgency is indispensable in the life of a committed Adventist, readiness for the advent is more a matter of character and life-style than emergency activity.

This life-style is that of the "faithful and wise servant" who provides, "at the proper time," day after day, food for the Lord's household. These faithful servants have what all men need—the truth about God and what His plans are for men. They win the favorable attention of those who thirst for peace of mind and hunger for solutions to human problems. Their words are compelling because their life-style is convincing. Such is a favorite theme of Ellen White: "A true, lovable Christian is the most powerful argument that can be advanced in favor of Bible truth. Such a man is Christ's representative. His life is the most convincing evidence that can be borne to the power of divine grace. When God's people bring the righteousness of Christ into the daily life, sinners will be converted and victories over the enemy will be gained."[1]

What kind of responsibility has the Lord of all people everywhere given to Christians, especially to Seventh-day Adventist Christians? What kind of nourishment are they, faithfully and wisely, to share with their fellowmen while they wait for their Lord to return?

Jesus clearly stated that the time of His return will depend upon when the church (His faithful servants) will have effectively proclaimed the "gospel of the kingdom"—for when a generation has had a fair opportunity to accept (or reject) His last message of mercy, "then the end will come." Matthew 24:14.

GOOD NEWS THAT JESUS REIGNS

This "gospel of the kingdom" is the good news of whatever Jesus has said, done, or will yet do. Good news of how Jesus reigns, how His kingdom is made up, is information not well known. But before time ends, this world will get a clear picture of what Jesus is doing about man's salvation. Making this good news known is the task of the "faithful and wise

THE END: THE UNIQUE VOICE OF ADVENTISTS

servant." This day-by-day nourishment—this living, convincing answer to humanity's biggest problems—provided by these faithful and wise servants at the end of time places the gospel of the kingdom before the world in living color. Such a message is far more than information that Jesus will return soon. The gospel is much more than a recital of biblical texts, repeated far and wide, in all languages, in every country of the world. The "gospel of the kingdom" is the good news that God has all the solutions for man's salvation, that Jesus reigns, especially in the lives of men and women of faith.

But who will believe it? This world has heard many solutions to human problems—many from Christian pulpits, often in contradiction. In many lives, cities and lands, Christianity has had its chance and, for many millions, failed. We refer to the "burned-over" lives, to post-Christian lands. For too many in the last quarter of the twentieth century, Christianity is a cloud without water.

How will God get His message across in such a world? Only a demonstration in flesh and blood can prove that God's kingly power can enable men and women to forsake selfish, self-destructive habits; that God's grace alone can ennoble men and women—equipping them to endure lovingly and convincingly under formidable pressures to retaliate or give up.[2]

Only flesh and blood can prove that the gospel is more than a theory. "The gospel of Christ is the law exemplified in character."[3] Jesus did it once and gave His church courage. But even His magnificent achievement as mankind's Substitute, Surety, and Example has been neutralized by bad theology down through the years. Even Jesus has become unconvincing for most of the world.

But this same Jesus will not condemn anyone or cause anyone to endure the dire consequences of the seven last plagues (Revelation 16) because he rejected a caricature fabricated by incorrect theology. Jesus will not close probation on the living until everyone has had enough correct information to make a fair, intelligent decision about Him as He really is.

WHAT JESUS WAITS FOR

Everyone in the last generation will have a fair chance to know what he is accepting or rejecting—when he accepts or rejects the truth.

Everyone will have the opportunity to decide whether God has been fair with him and the universe, whether He asks too much out of him in demanding obedience, whether there is real power available to live above selfishness and hate.[4]

The assignment of making this all clear to wondering heads and hearts has been given to the "faithful and wise servants," to "those who keep the commandments of God and the faith of Jesus." Revelation 14:12. The faithful and wise servant not only proclaims the word but encourages his neighbors with his life. Besides, he can explain how every man and woman can live that life too. Such a witness is believable because the life backs up the words spoken.[5]

The union of the life with the spoken testimony is an unbeatable fusion. Piety will surely not do the whole job—that has been tried many times. The spoken word has been tried times without number also with relatively little effectiveness. But when a person knows in his own experience that Jesus is truly his Saviour and without question provides pardon and power to overcome sin (Matthew 1:21), that person has a life and a testimony that cannot be hid any more than one can hide the sun from shining. "And they have conquered him by the blood of the Lamb and by the word of their testimony." Revelation 12:11. "For man believes with his heart and so is justified, and he confesses with his lips and so is saved." Romans 10:10.

Wherever his daily duties lead him, the "faithful and wise servant" is feeding the needs of those around him. When probation closes, where local conditions permit, he will be in the field or at the mill fulfilling his earthly responsibilities (Matthew 24:40, 41). The X-ray technician will be in his lab, the teacher in his classroom, the plumber with his pipes, the physician at the bedside, the student with his books, and the mother changing diapers. Discharging our earthly duties, in ways that reflect the glory of the character of God, is the "faithful and wise" servant's primary task. Such is the sense

THE END: THE UNIQUE VOICE OF ADVENTISTS

of sanctification: "True . . . sanctification consists of the cheerful performance of daily duties in perfect obedience to the will of God."[6]

A CREDIBLE BASE

Fulfilling our responsibilities as faithful fathers and mothers; as good neighbors; as responsive, trustworthy children; is the only possible base from which we can depart with literature, Bible studies, and sermons, to tell the world about the "good news of the kingdom" way of life—if we expect our words to be effective.[7] Reproducing the fruit of the Spirit (Galatians 5:22, 23), reflecting the character of Jesus in one's daily tasks, revealing the power of God that enables a person faithfully to do His will, is the statement of truth that the honest seekers will recognize. Note: "The Lord requires of all who profess to be His people, far more than they give Him. He expects believers in Christ Jesus to reveal to the world, in word and deed, the Christianity that was exemplified in the life and character of the Redeemer. If the Word of God is enshrined in their hearts, they will give a practical demonstration of the power and purity of the gospel. The testimony thus borne to the world is of much more value than sermons, or professions of godliness that do not reveal good works."[8]

The most that church machinery can do is to gain the attention of the world through the traditional forms of contact evangelism. (And so much more can yet be done.) Yet, after the seeker for truth has been pleasantly stopped and winsomely invited to take a look at Seventh-day Adventists, what then?

Here Ellen White incisively amplifies the harvest principle, "Character is power. The silent witness of a true, unselfish, godly life carries an almost irresistible influence. By revealing in our own life the character of Christ we cooperate with Him in the work of saving souls. It is only by revealing in our life His character that we can co-operate with Him. And the wider the sphere of our influence, the more good we may do. When those who profess to serve God follow Christ's example, practicing the principles of the law

WHAT JESUS WAITS FOR

in their daily life; when every act bears witness that they love God supremely and their neighbor as themselves, then will the church have power to move the world."[9]

This "power to move the world" is reflected in and through the daily behavior of the "faithful and wise servants" who "keep the commandments . . . and have the faith of Jesus."

THE WICKED SERVANT

Before we move to our Lord's second picture-story describing the faithful and wise servant who will have power to move the world, we should pause and listen to what Jesus says about the Adventists who are called "wicked servants"! "But if that wicked servant says to himself, 'My master is delayed,' and begins to beat his fellow servants, and eats and drinks with the drunken, the master of the servant will come on a day when he does not expect him and at an hour he does not know, and will punish him, and put him with the hypocrites; there men will weep and gnash their teeth." Matthew 24:48-51.

What a frightful end for those once committed to the Lord of the advent! What happened? The wicked servant says in his heart, "I still have time to get ready. I'll have my fling now, but when I see things shaping up, then I'll clean up my act. The end is not yet. After all, the Sunday law hasn't been passed. Furthermore, there are still countries in the world without the Adventist message, and there are more than 2000 groups yet without a Bible in their own language."

Either in spirit or word, the wicked servant, regardless of his good and regular standing as a church member, explains away the Lord's delay. Could it be that such Adventists, found unprepared when probation closes, will have lulled themselves into a false security by thinking that the delay in the advent is caused by some yet unfulfilled prophecy, some arbitrary time clock in the mind of God, and not the reluctance on the part of a significant number of the several generations since 1844 to receive into their lives the truths of the message of the three angels of Revelation 14? "For Christ's sake, His people should not add sin to sin by charging God with the consequence of their own wrong course of action."[10]

Returning to our Lord's emphasis on the kind of people who will be ready for His appearing, we note again that the parables of ten bridesmaids, the talents, and the judgment in Matthew 25 conclude Christ's answer to the question, "What will be the sign of your coming?" Matthew 24:3. Describing and amplifying the characteristics of the "faithful and wise servant," these three stories depict the kind of people found ready for probation to close in the last generation.

In general, the bridegroom parable describes two groups that have always existed in the Christian church—two groups bound together by common doctrines, representing members in "good and regular standing." Specificallly, the two groups of bridesmaids represent the conditions within the Seventh-day Adventist Church from 1844 to the advent.

The parable of the bridegroom employs the principle of the delayed advent. In fact, the experience of the ten maids, as they related to their responsibilities during the delay of the bridegroom, illustrates, according to Ellen White, "the experience of the church that shall live just before His second coming."[11]

The theme of the parable revolves around the delay of the bridegroom. The principle of the delayed advent is not an afterthought of Seventh-day Adventists. Not only is it an example of conditional prophecy (see chapter four), but the delay principle was built into the advent doctrine by Jesus Himself: "As the bridegroom was delayed." Matthew 25:5.

Both groups, the wise and foolish bridesmaids, represent Adventists at the end of time who expect Jesus to come in their day. Both groups "took their lamps and went to meet the bridegroom." Verse 1. Both groups possess and bear publicly their doctrinal lamps—all are church members. In fact, both groups are church-going Adventists. The difference between them lies not in the doctrine they believe about the return of Jesus (that is, they each possess a common lamp) but in what the doctrine has done for them personally.

An oil lamp is not worth much on a dark night without oil; a flashlight is useless without batteries. The lamp is merely an instrument, and its only purpose is to make something happen, that is, to produce light.

LIGHT IS CHARACTER

In this parable, as in life, the light is neither the lamp nor the oil. The light is not specifically biblical doctrine, no matter how pure or how much is known; nor is the Holy Spirit the light. The light is the witness of the Christlike life, transformed by the power of the Holy Spirit, molded by biblical principles. "Through the Holy Spirit, God's word is a light *as it* becomes a transforming power in the life of the receiver. By implanting in their hearts the principles of His word, the Holy Spirit develops in men the attributes of God. *The light of His glory—His character—is to shine forth in His followers.*"[12]

In other words, the five foolish bridesmaids were not shut out because their lamps were not as pretty, nor as big, as those of the five wise. They were unfit to be members of the wedding party, they could not participate in the work that had to be done, because their lamps were not producing light.

For Christians everywhere, the meaning is clear: the Bible-quoting church member (and we need more skilled Bible students) who has not been transformed by the Holy Spirit into a Christ-reflecting exhibit of the power of God is shutting himself out of the kingdom of God as well as delaying the advent. The five foolish church members have not received into their lives the intent of the messages of the three angels of Revelation 14; thus, they are unsuitable representations of Christ's way of life in those days when the gospel of His kingdom is to be preached with convincing effectiveness in all the world. It would not be safe to give them latter-rain power on earth—they would misrepresent God's kingdom. It would be unsafe to allow them into heaven—they were not overcomers.

Sad—sadder than words can tell—to realize that those who know the way are eventually lost! Sad it is to be so busy selling peanuts that one misses the parade.

The foolish bridesmaids are not lost because they couldn't answer doctrinal questions or didn't know enough Bible texts. We are told that "all have a knowledge of the Scriptures. All have heard the message of Christ's near approach, and confidently expect His appearing."[13]

The foolish bridesmaids are lost because they made biblical information an end, instead of a means to an end. The Bible did not become an instrument of faith but an object of faith. Faith became an intellectual exercise instead of a personal relationship of trusting obedience. They knew the Bible but not God as a personal friend.

The foolish bridesmaids can be compared to one who admires an expensive telescope. He hastens to make that telescope his own. He knows just where he wants to put that telescope to properly set it off—on his fireplace wall. He installs ceiling spotlights so that the silver filigree and the rich leather covering is properly appreciated. His neighbors, and soon his whole town, know about this wonderful telescope, so rare, so costly. Many are the nights his friends sit and admire it.

But hanging telescopes on fireplace walls misses the point of what a telescope is for. Telescopes are made to bring eternity into focus. Telescopes are made to see through—to catch the cadence of our Creator, to understand more clearly what God has on His mind for us to know. Telescopes are not made to look at, to embellish, but to see through.

The wise bridesmaids use the Bible to see what Isaiah saw, to hear what Paul heard—indeed its intended purpose. The Bible becomes the instrument by which faith is awakened, by which men and women are introduced to a self-authenticating relationship with their Lord. The result of this living experience, this listening to eternity, is a determined commitment on the part of the wise to say Yes to whatever God says, to make the principles set forth in the Bible the law of their lives by the power of the indwelling Spirit.

We have been warned: "It is not enough for us to believe that Jesus is not an impostor, and that the religion of the Bible is no cunningly devised fable. We may believe that the name of Jesus is the only name under heaven whereby man may be

WHAT JESUS WAITS FOR

saved, and yet we may not through faith make Him our personal Saviour. It is not enough to believe the theory of truth. It is not enough to make a profession of faith in Christ and have our names registered on the church roll. 'He that keepeth His commandments dwelleth in Him, and He in him. And hereby we know that He abideth in us, by the Spirit which He hath given us.' 'Hereby we do know that we know Him, if we keep His commandments.' 1 John 3:24; 2:3. This is the genuine evidence of conversion. Whatever our profession, it amounts to nothing unless Christ is revealed in works of righteousness."[14]

MISUNDERSTAND THE PURPOSE OF THE BIBLE

Misunderstanding the purpose of the Bible may well be one of the chief causes for the delay in the advent. Whenever the gospel becomes merely a proclamation of doctrine, and the encounter with an empowering, sin-removing Saviour becomes muted, then something very alien to the New Testament has taken over.

Doctrinal understanding alone does not produce industrious, diligent workers; peaceful, forbearing church members; alert, loving parents. For example, most every child, in either Sunday School or Sabbath School, was taught early that "A soft answer turns away wrath." Proverbs 15:1. No question about it, that memory verse has been repeated often. But does the lamp produce light? Does that Bible text become inbedded within the habit pattern? Has the church member discovered that more often than not, difficult as it may be at times, "a soft answer" does change the climate, it does indeed close great rifts? Not always, because even Jesus did not turn away all wrath—but for the most part it works. The Bible becomes a light, a glory light reflecting God's character when one asks the Holy Spirit to transform biblical principles into human behavior.

In times of ease, the wise and foolish may have been difficult to distinguish. After all, both slept during the delay. But the wise woke up, they sensed the emptiness of their spiritual experience, and they determined to change by the grace of God. When emergencies came, they were better prepared. When children needed counsel, their preception and wisdom were equal to the task. When neighbors were troubled, appropriate words, born in intensive preparation, were given. When disaster struck, the deep calm of a tested friendship with Jesus provided new strength for all.

But when emergencies struck the foolish church members, they behaved like anyone else who knew nothing about the Bible. Because they had been leaning on others to supply their strength for so long, they now were spiritually anemic without a chance for recovery. They were too far gone for a blood transfusion. They discovered too late that courage, peace, trust, and strength of spirit could not be transferred.

Just as no one can breathe for another, so no one can trust for another. Or say Yes for another. Even God will not give, posit, reckon, or credit His character to another in the judgment. "Character is not transferable."[15] The Bible-quoting church member untransformed by the Holy Spirit into a Christ-reflecting man or woman will not be ready for probation to close. Such will not be safe to save. Somewhere in the life the person is still saying No to God. He is not acting on the truth that he knows. He is a rebel. And no angel will permit such a person to enter heaven. How sad to observe that men and women "are shut out from heaven by their own unfitness for its companionship."[16]

The wise bridesmaid is our Lord's "faithful and wise servant." The transformed Christian is the only witness to the world that Jesus is a living Lord, a powerful Intercessor in the battle with evil.[17] Such faithful and wise servants are the only evidence that Christianity is worth accepting, that the God Christians talk about actually can do all that they say He can. Transformed Christians, sealed by the Holy Spirit, are very much involved in the decision making of millions in the last generation. They represent the gospel which all honest people will have to accept or reject.[18]

MORE THAN PROCLAIMING THE SABBATH

The message of Seventh-day Adventists is more than proclaiming which day of the week is the Sabbath of the fourth commandment. "Receiving the third angel's message" (a

WHAT JESUS WAITS FOR

phrase dear to Seventh-day Adventists) is more than worshiping on the seventh day of the week.

The message of the Seventh-day Adventist Church is a call to take God seriously, to live like Jesus by the same grace He depended on,[19] to have faith as He had,[20] to allow Jesus to be "glorified in them." John 17:10. What Jesus was to do for truth, so His followers are to do: "As thou didst send me into the world, so I have sent them into the world." John 17:18.

For this sober reason Ellen White etches deeply the challenge: "So the followers of Christ are to shed light into the darkness of the world. . . . The light of His glory—His character—is to shine forth in His followers. Thus they are to glorify God, to lighten the path to the Bridegroom's home, to the city of God, to the marriage supper of the Lamb. . . .

"It is the darkness of misapprehension of God that is enshrouding the world. Men are losing their knowledge of His character. It has been misunderstood and misinterpreted. At this time a message from God is to be proclaimed, a message illuminating in its influence and saving in its power. His character is to be made known. Into the darkness of the world is to be shed the light of His glory, the light of His goodness, mercy, and truth. . . .

"The last rays of merciful light, the last message of mercy to be given to the world, is a revelation of His character of love. The children of God are to manifest His glory. In their own life and character they are to reveal what the grace of God has done for them.

"The light of the Sun of Righteousness is to shine forth in good works—in words of truth and deeds of holiness."[21]

In summary: God's faithful commandment keepers—pictured as the "faithful and wise servant" and the wise bridesmaid—become a light to all honest seekers for truth in word and behavior; the light brings sense and urgency to all on the verge of the kingdom, motivating them to want this life-style for their own. These loyal believers are God's faithful representatives; they are safe to save. As Ellen White said, they have a right to enter the circle of the redeemed: "When those who claim to be children of God become Christ-like in character, they will be obedient to

THE END: THE UNIQUE VOICE OF ADVENTISTS

God's commandments. Then the Lord can trust them to be of the number who shall compose the family of heaven. . . . They have a right to join the blood-washed throng. . . .

"Those who reject the gift of Christ's righteousness are rejecting the attributes of character which would constitute them the sons and daughters of God. They are rejecting that which alone could give them a fitness for a place at the marriage feast."[22]

PARABLE OF PROFITABLE SERVANT

How does the last-day seeker for truth mature into this kind of a person? To answer this question, Jesus told the story of the talents, or perhaps more accurately, the story of the profitable servants.

The parable of the profitable servants adds to the description Jesus gave of the "faithful and wise servant" who represents those who are ready for the close of probation and the advent. In a specific sense this parable, or snapshot, states the principle that should motivate the life of every Seventh-day Adventist during the time of the delayed advent. Though this parable has been valuable for centuries, it has had special application since 1844. "He showed what it means to watch for His coming. The time is to be spent, not in idle waiting, but in diligent working. This lesson He taught in the parable of the talents."[23] Our Lord's message in this parable should lead every Christian to say, "This is the kind of person I want to be."

Before we can understand the parable we must define what is meant by "talents." In our Lord's story, the talent was a specific amount of money. More talents were given to those who had the experience and initiative to handle large responsibilities for their employer. Those who had less skills, for whatever reason, received less financial responsibility. All received as much as they could safely handle. As time went by, as each employee grew in ability to handle opportunities to be responsible and useful, the employer would gladly give each faithful employee more talents to match greater abilities. Responsibility (talents) was keyed to each person's ability (natural and acquired) to handle it.[24]

WHAT JESUS WAITS FOR

In applying the parable to the Christian life, we may define a talent as a certain level of opportunity and responsibility to serve and to grow. Many talents given means much ability is recognized and—on that basis—hard, heavy work is commensurately assigned. The dominant purpose of the parable then is to teach that the "true object of life is ministry"; that the "law of service" is the way to personality fulfillment as well as the way to fulfill God's will.

But, someone may ask, how does this all work out in a practical way? What does this have to do with hastening the advent? How does this parable relate to the "faithful and wise servant" and to the kind of person who becomes a wise bridesmaid?

In context, this parable follows the parable of the bridegroom and the ten bridesmaids, which teaches that the mature Christian, the Christ-reflecting church member, is the key to preaching the gospel of the kingdom in the last days. The five wise bridesmaids represent those within the church who finally demonstrate what the Holy Spirit can do when given full opportunity. The light that the Bridegroom needs before He can return is His glory—His character—reflected in transformed, Christlike church members.

The parable of the profitable employees supplements the parable of the bridegroom and the bridesmaids—it explains how all this light-producing, Christ-reflecting demonstration can be accomplished.

SELF-DEVELOPMENT, OUR FIRST GOAL

This leads us to the fundamental theme of the parable—that one thought every Christian must face sooner or later: Our first duty to God and man is self-development.[25] This is a very sobering thought, a crushing thought, for the self-indulgent or for those who want Jesus to forgive their sins but not really to save them from their sins.

Elsewhere in the Bible, the goal of self-development, the purpose of the Christian harvest, is set forth as the stature of Jesus Christ. See Ephesians 4:13-24. The parable of the profitable employees is one more expression of the harvest principle.

THE END: THE UNIQUE VOICE OF ADVENTISTS

For many, some of the most inspiring thoughts in all literature were penned by Ellen White while expanding on this theme of self-development as man's first duty to God and man.

She speaks of moral perfection and how no sincere Christian will lower the standards he must reach in order to accommodate inherited or cultivated tendencies to self-indulgence and wrongdoing.[26]

She shows how physical and mental habits have much to do with moral perfection. "Our impulses and passions have their seat in the body, and it must be kept in the best condition physically and under the most spiritual influences in order that our talents may be put to the highest use.

"Anything that lessens physical strength enfeebles the mind and makes it less capable of discriminating between right and wrong. We become less capable of choosing the good and have less strength of will to do that which we know to be right. . . .

"The physical life is to be carefully preserved and developed that through humanity the divine nature may be revealed in its fulness."[27]

She emphasizes the continual call to mental excellence: "He designs that His servants shall possess more intelligence and clearer discernment than the worldling, and He is displeased with those who are too careless or too indolent to become efficient, well-informed workers."[28]

The great problems of the human family and their solutions—philosophic, economic, religious, or any other area—should not be left for only the children of this world to grapple with. It is one thing to serve humanity by being their bootblacks and laundrymaids (and such tasks are eminently useful), or for Christians to meet their neighbors at their back doors, or even front porches. It is something else to be invited through the front doors, and to sit with them in the parlor as teachers and instruments of grace.

Especially does Ellen White emphasize that an intellectual Christian can love and serve God best. This does not mean that only those church members with a graduate degree in theology have an inside track to heaven. But she does em-

WHAT JESUS WAITS FOR

phasize that God "lays upon us the obligation of developing the intellect to its fullest capacity, that with all the mind we may know and love our Creator."[29]

All of this involves the right use of our time, speech habits, money and influence, the concern for accuracy, the willingness to take advice, and everything else that will improve us wherever we are, in whatever line of work we may engage.

RELATION TO HASTENING THE ADVENT

The question may yet linger: What does all this have to do with hastening the advent? Self-development is the only way that a person can be ready for the call to service. No person is excluded. Everyone has some ability to love and serve—everyone has, relatively speaking, one talent of opportunity and matching ability. Our response to the daily call to service is the test of our fitness to live forever. It reveals how much we know about love.

The daily task of being a person, in relation to other persons, gives us all an unending call to serve. But no one learns, for example, how to be a thoughtful, caring parent overnight. If a parent is not preparing for the searching questions and self-asserting independence of a fifteen-year-old son or daughter, he will never be ready for the surprises. Self-development for the parent means that he or she learns everything possible about child development and about basic problems that concern perceptive young people. A prepared parent is the truly loving parent, the parent that young people can trust as well as formally respect.

The nurse or physician who does not do his homework well, who memorizes only to pass the next test, who doesn't reach out for the latest research—will rarely be the cool, adept human solution to desperate medical emergencies. Self-development is the route to genuine service. Self-development is the only habit pattern that truly loves.

Helping the Lord of the universe to demonstrate what the power of God can do for sin-spoiled persons is one aspect of the Christian's self-development. Another is that increasing one's ability to be ready for all emergencies and opportunities in life makes the Christian a modern representative of Jesus Christ—an exhibit of love and concern. Need it be emphasized that the growing, self-developing Christian is the happiest, friendliest person in the neighborhood?

Not only are we to be willing to be useful, we are to do something definite about improving ouselves so that we indeed can be useful when the occasion arises. What a pity that so many are sympathetic with another's need, whether it be physical distress, spiritual depression, or moral weakness, and yet are not able to do something substantial in relief! The "faithful and wise servant" is not the friend or parent who wrings his hands in the face of another's needs; he is the prepared servant who can shed light along the way, who can relieve human distress as God uses him to comfort the troubled.

The Holy Spirit assists the "faithful and wise servant," the wise bridesmaid, the profitable servant, in two ways: He empowers him daily to improve and to persevere in the work of self-development; and when men and women, at times, meet opportunities beyond their natural abilities, the Spirit is ready and pleased to supplement man's capacities with the "gifts of the Spirit." To have great human resources is not enough. Good works without the Spirit can probably be done for a while, but either base motives or inconsistency will soon be revealed.

The best part of our Lord's description of his maturing followers is that no man or woman is pegged forever at any level. Those able to handle five talents worth of opportunity and responsibility will get more added on, if they are faithful; men and women given one talent of responsibility can and will grow to two, to five, and only God knows what the limit is. No person has ever reached his limits! God does not "supernaturally endow us with the qualifications we lack; but while we use that which we have, He will work with us to increase and strengthen every faculty."[30]

But every coin has two sides. Charlie Brown and Lucy were taking a walk with Snoopy. Lucy speaks: "Sooner or later, Charlie Brown, there's one thing you're going to have to learn. . . . You reap what you sow! You get out of life exactly what you put into it! No more and no less!" They

WHAT JESUS WAITS FOR

walk on in deep thought. Then Snoopy makes a comment—"I'd like to see a little more margin for error."

Snoopy's response reflects a moan that has arisen in every generation since our first parents left the Garden. It is heard throughout the pages of literature. Jesus mirrored this pitiful plea in this parable. Even God, because He chooses not to, will not alter the law of seed sowing. He chooses a predictable universe, an uncoerced kingdom of willing sons and daughters—they will reap what they sow.

Jesus said, "Take the talent from him, and give it to him who has the ten talents. For to every one who has will more be given, and he will have abundance; but from him who has not, even what he has will be taken away." Matthew 25:28, 29.

No question about it, God will help reverse the life direction of anyone who asks Him to plant and cultivate the gospel seed in his life. But the individual must choose what seed is to be planted and cultivated—wheat or tares. God can not, will not, force the growth of gospel seed where it is unwelcome.

DIRE CONSEQUENCES TO REBEL

Dire consequences are promised the man who refused to accept ever-increasing opportunities to grow, to serve, and to develop his moral, mental, physical, and social powers. He goes on record before all the universe as one determined to do things his way. He proves to all that he would be unfit to save. He has made a habit out of being a rebel, he refuses to cooperate with the great laws of life. He made a deeply etched practice of saying No when he should have been saying Yes to God. That person is not a "faithful and wise servant," not a wise bridesmaid.

The sad part of this parable, and thus about life as it will be played out in the last generation, is that the man or woman who will be finally rejected, the person who played it cool and just rocked along, was an acceptable church member. He was not an open sinner. His sin was not some great evil or hate. His great sin was what he had not done for himself and for others. He rebelled against the law of self-development. He closed up his own probation. Although he did no great evil, he will be judged with the crowd outside the gates of the holy city.

They will plead their inability; they will point to others who had more opportunities; they will cry that they never had the breaks. But whatever lack of ability they bemoan was caused by their own inactivity—even as a muscle gets very weak when not in use. In real life, the imprudent employees may be five-talent people as well as those of one talent. Many five-talent people will be lost because they, like the "wicked and slothful servant," buried their abilities and shunned their opportunities. They turned down the volume until they could not hear the Holy Spirit urging them on. They became comfortable without the Holy Spirit—they had tuned Him out. And did not feel guilty anymore. For them probation closed. Snoopy is right—"there's not much margin for error." No one drifts into the kingdom of God. Continual rebelling against the law of self-development merely hastens the day when those sad words are heard, "Take the talent from him."

The parable of the talents is not all demand and task and work. If Jesus were to stop here, He would be laying an impossible burden on our back. He would be asking for more than we could deliver. It would be a depressing message to ask for continual improvement, even perfection, as if it were only a matter of self-development. The gospel is not only demand and obligation and requirement. Such would be legalism in new dress and just as futile as old Israel's attempt to reach righteousness by works.

An essential part of the gospel, that puts fresh air into our flat tires, is the news that God never gives a task without an assurance that "all His biddings are enablings."[31] With the obligations come the gifts—all parts of the gospel treasure. God does not ask the impossible nor the unreasonable. He knows how weak we are, how pressed we may become. So He promised, "The heavenly intelligences will work with the human agent who seeks with determined faith that perfection of character which will reach out to perfection in action."[32]

But Jesus is not yet finished as He completes His portrait of the "faithful and wise servant." He knew better! If He

WHAT JESUS WAITS FOR

stopped with the parable of the talents, or the story of the profitable servants, the thought could linger that the best Christian is the great achiever, the genius—he who is the most brilliant, the most physically fit. The bronzed, muscular beachboys and the slim slenderellas would be close to the kingdom.

Self-development—no question. No real service is done without a prepared man or woman. We can give only what we have. Peter's outreach to the beggar is still true: "Silver and gold have I none; but such as I have give I thee." Acts 3:6, K.J.V. Self-development must always be the reflection of the Good Samaritan—and this leads us to Christ's last picture story describing the kind of people who represent the harvest of the gospel seed in the last generation.

TO THOSE WHO KNOW HOW TO LOVE

Our Lord's last snapshot—that of the sheep and the goats—reminds us that fulfilling the goal of genuine Christianity (call it maturity, moral perfection, or righteousness produced by faith) is primarily in the world of being, far beyond the world of only knowing, or even doing "good" works. This, the five foolish Adventist bridesmaids and the self-serving, talent-burying employees learned too late.

The conditions for belonging to the group on "his right hand," for those who are fit to live forever, are not beyond the reach of anyone. Here we see that righteousness is not granted as a diploma after years of hard study or as a certificate for baptizing 100 persons annually, necessary and commendable as these achievements are. Entrance into the kingdom of God is not for those who merely kept the rules, maintained the standards, and answered all the questions with the right answers. But a wide and glorious welcome will be extended to those who know how to love freely and spontaneously.

The "faithful and wise servant," the wise bridesmaid, the profitable employee have directed their lives around one principle—the turning point in the judgment—the law of loving service. In the judgment, our Lord's decision turns "upon one point. When the nations are gathered before Him, there will be but two classes, and their eternal destiny will be determined by what they have done or have neglected to do for Him in the person of the poor and the suffering. In that day Christ does not present before men the great work He has done for them in giving His life for their redemption. He presents the faithful work they have done for Him."[33]

Such faithful and wise servants reflect the glory of His own earthly experience. They may not, in many cases, know much theology; but they have coveted opportunities to serve, to lift the distressed, to cheer the downhearted, to help right the wrongs done to those who have been mistreated. But the self-absorbed, the self-indulgent, become unconscious of these opportunities—and thus their guilt—because they have permitted Satan to blind them.

This last snapshot of "those who keep the commandments of God and the faith of Jesus" (Revelation 14:12) clears the air. Righteousness is not only accepting what Jesus has done for us; righteousness also includes what we permit Jesus, through the Holy Spirit, to do in and through us. Such Christians are not frightened into righteousness, because only the loving person is a righteous person. Only a loving person fulfills the law. Romans 13:10.

Love in action is the word that sums up the life-style of the faithful and wise servant who is ready, day and night, in season and out, with whatever his fellowmen need. Christlike love, the absence of self-gratification and moral rebellion, sums up the life-style of the wise bridesmaids who day in and day out had developed a character pattern that could be relied on in all emergencies. Love is the motivating principle behind the total effort of those committed persons who developed natural abilities and enlarged their opportunities to serve—they did it always for the sake of others. They didn't want to be caught empty-handed in the face of someone else's need.

The fully committed Christian is a living demonstration of the fact that "when self is merged in Christ, love springs forth spontaneously. The completeness of Christian character is attained when the impulse to help and bless others springs constantly from within—when the sunshine of heaven fills the heart and is revealed in the countenance."[34]

Genuine Christian love is never turned inward—such would be a contradiction of terms. Rather than an inordinate preoccupation with self-examination, love is mission-oriented—always turned outward and prepared to do and say what Jesus would do for anyone needing healing of body, mind, or soul.

ONLY ANSWER TO MISSIONARY IMPULSE

Love is the motivating force that turns the last-day Christians to men and women everywhere—beginning with the neighborhood and reaching to the ends of the earth. All other hitherto concerns and self-interests are finally placed in proper perspective as God's people in the last generation rise to their opportunities.

Spontaneous love—the habitual, predictable life pattern of mature Christians—is the only acceptable motivation for self-development, and the only proper motivation for evangelism. Only when the Christian witness truly loves in a full-orbed commitment of mind, body, social responsibilities, and time will his message be judged credible—no matter how many men and women are baptized or confronted with the preached Word.

Loving people know that it is not always easy to love. Loving people guard their health so that they do not become ill and thus a burden on someone else. Loving people take time to do their homework—such as first-aid classes, Bible-study seminars, and discussion groups—so that they will be ready when opportunities arise. Loving people work at settling the deep questions, and do not drift, because they know that only those firmly convinced about what is truth can ever convince someone else.

Nothing more can be expected from anyone than "the completeness of Christian character." This kind of life pattern, as depicted in Matthew 24 and 25, will settle many questions in the great controversy and will open the way for Jesus to return. This kind of people can be trusted to live forever because they have demonstrated, not only a habit pattern that has become etched into their nervous system by

THE END: THE UNIQUE VOICE OF ADVENTISTS

the Holy Spirit, but a posture toward God that will always say Yes to whatever He wills. Rebellion is gone forever.[35] Consistent and uncontrived, mature Christians reflect faithfully the life of Jesus. They would be safe to save. All other worlds could be safely exposed to them. Truth has settled so deeply into their lives that sin will never arise again.[36]

References

1. Ellen G. White, *Review and Herald*, January 14, 1904.
2. Emil Brunner said it well, "The Ekklesia [church] has to bear a double witness to Christ, through the *Word* that tells of what He has bestowed upon it, and through the witness of its *life*, through its being, which points to Him as its vital source.

"These two testimonies of the Ekklesia through Word and life corroborate each other, and neither is fully effective without the other. The Word of Christ is truly effective and credible only where it is accompanied by the life-witness of the Ekklesia. . . .

"The gospel of Christ is a Word 'from faith to faith'—more precisely, a Word from the fellowship of faith leading to the fellowship of faith, and for this reason it is credible only where it is accompanied by the life witness of the Ekklesia. Without this it is unintelligible, unworthy of belief. When it is not backed by the love of those who speak it, it is a self-contradiction." *The Christian Doctrine of the Church, Faith, and the Consummation* (Philadelphia: The Westminster Press, 1962), pp. 134, 135.
3. Ellen G. White, *Selected Messages*, bk. 2, p. 108.
4. "In like manner the disciples of Christ are set as light-bearers on the way to heaven; through them the Father's mercy and goodness are made manifest to a world enshrouded in the darkness of misapprehension of God. By seeing their good works, others are led to glorify the Father who is above; for it is made manifest that there is a God on the throne of the universe whose character is worthy of praise and imitation. The divine love glowing in the heart, the Christlike harmony manifested in the life, are as a glimpse of heaven granted to men of the world. . . . The world watches to see what fruit is borne by professed Christians. It has a right to look for self-denial and self-sacrifice from those who claim to believe advanced truth. . . .

"God has ordained that His work shall be presented to the world in distinct, holy lines. He desires His people to show by their lives the advantage of Christianity over worldliness. By His grace every provision has been made for us in all our transaction of business to demonstrate the superiority of heaven's principles over the principles of the world. We are to show that we are working upon a higher plane than that of worldliness. In all things we are to manifest purity of character, to show that the truth received and obeyed makes the receivers sons and daughters of God, children of the heavenly King, and that as such they are honest in their dealings, faithful, true, and upright in the small as well as the great things of life."—White, *Review and Herald,* July 27, 1905.

5. "The world to-day is in crying need of a revelation of Christ Jesus in the person of His saints. God desires that His people shall stand before the world a holy people. Why?—Because there is a world to be saved by the light of gospel truth; and as the message of truth that is to call men out darkness into God's marvelous light, is given by the church, the lives of its members, sanctified by the Spirit of truth, are to bear witness to the verity of the messages proclaimed. . . .

"The world is in need of a demonstration of practical Christianity. In view of the fact that those who claim to be followers of Christ are a spectacle to an unbelieving world, it behooves them to make sure that they are in right relation with God. . . . In order to stand as lights in the world, they need to have the clear light of the Sun of Righteousness constantly shining upon them. . . .

"When God's people so fully separate themselves from evil that He can let the light of heaven rest upon them in rich measure, and shine forth from them to the world, then there will be fulfilled, more fully than it has ever been fulfilled in the past, the prophecy of Isaiah, . . . 'The Gentiles shall come to thy light, and kings to the brightness of thy rising. . . . The abundance of the sea shall be converted unto thee, the forces of the Gentiles shall come unto thee' (Isaiah 60:3-5).—White, *Review and Herald,* March 31, 1910.

6. White, *Christ's Object Lessons,* p. 360.

7. "What preaching isolated from the fellowship of the Ekklesia is no longer able to achieve, to bring men in contact with Christ, can perhaps be achieved by the Christian fellowship which does not at first utter its witness to Christ aloud. Differently put: this genuine Ekklesia, which as such is both fellowship with Christ and brotherhood, will realize that because of the century-long separation of faith and love, of fellowship with Christ and human fellowship, the way to win the men of today is not at first to speak the message of Christ, but merely to *live* it. This would be a reversal of the hitherto customary way from faith to active love. And that would mean: not first preaching and Bible study, but first genuine disinterested service of our neighbours, and only afterwards—when the other person asks 'Why are you so different and why do you act so differently from the others?—the witness to Christ, the revealer of the love of God and the founder of true loving service of our fellow men."—Emil Brunner, *The Christian Doctrine of the Church,* p. 115.

8. Ellen G. White Comments in *S.D.A. Bible Commentary,* vol. 4, p. 1181.

9. White, *Christ's Object Lessons,* p. 340. "As you advance heavenward, make use of every common, every-day habit and custom to illustrate truth, and in every calling, however menial, live out the life of Christ. In this way you will be to men a continual revelation of what Christ would

have men be in your position. . . .

"Truth is to be communicated from one human agent to another and to be molded into the life and character of those who receive it, in order that glory may redound to God. Truth that has found its proper setting, flashes brilliant rays of divine light into darkened minds, and meets the wants and necessities of the minds and hearts of fallen men who could not be reached by any other agency. It is by living out the truth in human life that souls are to be reached. As the Son of God in human form was perfect in his life, so he requires that his followers shall be perfect in their lives. He was made in all things like unto his brethren. . . . In living out the truth of God, man is continually assured that supernatural help will be granted to him, and that while he retains his human nature, yet through an unseen agency he receives the impress of the divine nature through the truth as it is in Jesus."—White, *Review and Herald,* October, 23, 1894.

10. White, *Evangelism* (Washington, D.C.: Review and Herald Publishing Association, 1946), p. 696.

11. White, *Christ's Object Lessons,* p. 406. "I am often referred to the parable of the ten virgins. . . . This parable has been and will be fulfilled to the very letter, for it has a special application to this time."—White, *Review and Herald,* August 19, 1890.

12. White, *Christ's Object Lessons,* p. 414 (italics supplied).

13. *Ibid.,* p. 408.

14. *Ibid.,* p. 312, 313.

15. *Ibid.,* p. 412. When a sinner is pardoned, Christ's character stands in place of the pardoned sinner's character; he is regarded as if he had not sinned. But God intends more than forgiveness and a "clean slate" for those Christ will save "from their sins." Matthew 1:21. If the believer cooperates, Christ will change the heart so that, by His power within, the believer "will manifest the same spirit and do the same good works" that Jesus revealed. See Ellen G. White, *Steps to Christ* (Mountain View, Calif.: Pacific Press Publishing Association), pp. 62, 63. The sincerity of the believer is tested by his attitude toward sin and toward Christ's efforts to help him overcome all inherited and cultivated tendencies to evil. In the judgment (Matthew 7:21-27; 25:31-46) the issue is character: how loyal and reliable, how predictably loving, has the believer become by the grace of God. At that time Christ will decide who are worthy, judging every man according to his words and his works. Each person's character will determine his destiny. See White, *Christ's Object Lessons,* p. 72.

16. *Ibid.,* p. 413.

17. "Everyone who will break from the slavery and service of Satan, and will stand under the blood-stained banner of Prince Immanuel will be kept by Christ's intercessions. Christ, as our Mediator, at the right hand of the Father, ever keeps us in view, for it is as necessary that He should keep us by His intercessions as that He should redeem us with His blood. If He lets go His hold of us for one moment, Satan stands ready to destroy. Those purchased by His blood, He now keeps by His intercession." Ellen G. White Comments, *S.D.A. Bible Commentary,* vol. 6, p. 1078.

WHAT JESUS WAITS FOR

"God loved the world so dearly that He gave his only-begotten Son that whosoever would accept Him might have power to live His righteous life. Christ proved that it is possible for man to lay hold by faith on the power of God."—White, *Selected Messages*, bk. 1, p. 223.

18. See White, *Testimonies*, vol. 6, p. 11.
19. See Ellen G. White, *Acts of the Apostles* (Mountain View, Calif.: Pacific Press Publishing Association, 1911), p. 56; White, *The Desire of Ages*, p. 73; Ellen G. White Comments, *S.D.A. Bible Commentary*, vol. 5, p. 1123.
20. See author's *Faith, Saying Yes to God* (Nashville, Tenn.: Southern Publishing Association, 1978), pp. 11-13; White, *The Desire of Ages*, pp. 389, 679, 680, 756.
21. White, *Christ's Object Lessons*, pp. 414-416.
22. *Ibid.*, pp. 315, 316.
23. *Ibid.*, p. 325.
24. *Ibid.*, p. 328.
25. *Ibid.*, p. 329.
26. *Ibid.*, pp. 330-333.
27. *Ibid.*, pp. 346, 348.
28. *Ibid.*, p. 333.
29. *Ibid.*, p. 333. "Only by a continual improvement of the intellectual as well as the moral powers can we hope to answer the purpose of our Creator. God is displeased with those who are too careless or indolent to become efficient, well-informed workers. The Christian should possess more intelligence and keener discernment than the worldling."—White, *Testimonies*, vol. 4, p. 545.
30. White, *Christ's Object Lessons*, pp. 353, 354.
31. *Ibid.*, p. 333.
32. *Ibid.*, p. 332, 112.
33. Ellen G. White, *The Desire of Ages*, p. 637.
34. White, *Christ's Object Lessons*, p. 384.
35. See the author's *Faith, Saying Yes to God*, pp. 85-95.
36. "Just as soon as the people of God are sealed in their foreheads—it is not any seal or mark that can be seen, but a settling into the truth, both intellectually and spiritually, so they cannot be moved—just as soon as God's people are sealed and prepared for the shaking, it will come."—Ellen G. White Comments on Ezekiel 9:2-4, *S.D.A. Bible Commentary*, vol. 4, p. 1161.

Between Now and Then

Seventh-day Adventists are not only advent-oriented; they are last-day-events-oriented. Over the years, charts, diagrams, and sequences of last-day events have been compared and studied, and rightly so. Paul set the tempo when he wrote: "But you are not in darkness, brethren, for that day to surprise you like a thief. For you are all sons of light and sons of the day; we are not of the night or of darkness. So then let us not sleep, as others do, but let us keep awake and be sober. . . . Therefore encourage one another and build one another up, just as you are doing." 1 Thessalonians 5:4-6, 11.

One of Adventism's key writers wrote: "So in the prophecies the future is opened before us as plainly as it was opened to the disciples by the words of Christ. The events connected with the close of probation and the work of preparation for the time of trouble, are clearly presented."[1]

As we have said earlier, we must continue to distinguish between events that have already transpired, or have always been part of the world scene in varying intensities, and those events unequivocally connected with the last days and/or yet to be fulfilled. We are told that we have "a chart pointing out every waymark on the heavenward journey" and we "ought not to guess at anything."[2]

OUGHT NOT TO GUESS

What can be known about "closing events"? What is indisputable among Adventists and what is debatable? Naturally, some will place more items into a particular category than others would. But generally speaking, the following summary will perhaps be affirmed by the majority.

In broad strokes, biblical writers have given us a panorama that will help identify the landscape of the last days. In several lines of development Daniel outlined the course of world history up to the second advent. The land area once known as the Roman Empire would remain unfederated until the second advent. Daniel 2. The papacy would function as a world power until the second advent. Daniel 7. The papacy will continue until "by no human hand, he shall be broken" (Daniel 8:25) in the judgments of God just prior to the second advent. In 1844, at the close of the 2300-day (year) prophecy, a movement arises that begins the clarification and restoration of the truth about how God saves men and women. Daniel 8. The papacy will extend its world influence by political means; it is perceived as instrumental in solving many world tensions until its designs are unmasked and "he shall come to his end, with none to help him." Daniel 11.[3] Daniel 12 notes that the prophecies of Daniel would be obscure until the time of the end. At that time "knowledge shall increase" regarding the closing events of history as predicted in Daniel. "The time of trouble" will precede the advent, during which time there will be a special resurrection.

Jesus foretold world conditions prior to His advent in Matthew 24. We have already discussed some of His counsel as recorded in Matthew 24 and 25 in chapter seven of this book. In summary, from the first century until the second advent there will be false Christs, wars, famines, and earthquakes. The bleak conclusion, one that mankind has repeatedly rejected in favor of a more optimistic view, is that this world is not going to get better. The end will come when the gospel has been truly preached throughout the whole world. Signs in the heavenly bodies will be specific events, pinpointing the nearness of the advent. But open disdain and unconcern, similar to the response given to Noah, will characterize most people in the last days.

Luke's account of Christ's last-day predictions adds certain features, such as the distress of nations at the roaring of the sea and waves, and men fainting with fear and foreboding regarding world events. Luke 21:25-27.

Paul was given several previews of last-day events. The world will scorn the warning of the advent and live as though all problems then besetting society would be solved sooner or later. 1 Thessalonians 5:2-4. The papacy will develop into a world power and reach its zenith shortly before the second advent. 2 Thessalonians 2.

In Paul's second letter to Timothy, he again refers to the insidious dangers facing the church in his own day and which would continue to threaten the purity of the church until Christ returned. Chapter 3:1-5.

THE REVELATION OF JOHN

John the revelator seems to give the fullest picture of the end times. In Revelation 6 the sixth seal appears to amplify the signs in the celestial bodies given by Jesus in Matthew 24. In Revelation 13 the papacy is pictured as a world power that received a deadly wound and yet reemerges as a world power in the last days; and the United States plays a critical role in last-day events, especially when individual freedoms wane during the collapse of constitutional safeguards.

Revelation 14 depicts a global movement under the symbolism of three angels. The first angel represents a worldwide mission program which emphasizes the urgency of the judgment hour. Central to its message is that the Judge of all men is the Creator of the world. The second angel warns that religions generally have had their day and that all honest men and women must examine their relationship to "fallen" religious systems. The third angel sponsors a worldwide appeal for all honest seekers of truth to join those people who keep the commandments of God and the faith of Jesus.

The "seven last plagues" are described in Revelation 16, events that transpire following the close of probation. The awesome characteristics of the papacy, especially in the last days, are delineated in Revelation 17. The closing moments of an effectively proclaimed gospel, through Christ-reflecting church members, are described in Revelation 18. God's part in the sixth and seventh plagues, the closing scenes of a united world against commandment keepers in the battle of Armageddon, are set forth in Revelation 16 and 19.

Although we have followed broad strokes, Christians are always wise to use caution and suspended judgment when filling in the details of unfulfilled prophecy. After all, we are not prophets—merely students of prophecy. James White gave his church some sound advice: "In exposition of unfulfilled prophecy, where the history is not written, the student should put forth his propositions with not too much positiveness, lest he find himself straying in the field of fancy. There are those who think more of future truth than of present truth. They see but little light in the path in which they walk, but think they see great light ahead of them."[4]

UNFULFILLED CONDITIONS

When we turn to those events that must transpire within the large framework we have just depicted, we are reminded again that if Jesus could have come before 1880 (any date during the generation that lived in 1844 would do) no specific Bible prophecy remains unfulfilled,[5] except those which are consequences of certain unfulfilled conditions relating to the maturity of God's people.

The fact that these conditions regarding the state of God's people are unfulfilled has been kept before Seventh-day Adventists for over a century.[6] These conditions are all elements in the harvest principle; they represent the contingencies that affect the time when Jesus decides that the "harvest is ripe."

THE SEAL OF GOD

The first condition is that Christ's followers must have the "seal of God" (Revelation 7:1-4; 14:1-5; Ezekiel 9:4) before they can receive "the latter rain." "Not one of us will ever receive the seal of God while our characters have one spot or stain upon them. It is left with us to remedy the defects in our characters, to cleanse the soul temple of every defilement. Then the latter rain will fall upon us as the early rain fell upon the disciples on the Day of Pentecost."[7]

The seal of God is Heaven's seal of approval upon the Christlike life. "The seal of the living God will be placed upon those only who bear a likeness to Christ in character."[8] "Those who receive the seal of the living God and are protected in the time of trouble must reflect the image of Jesus

THE END: THE UNIQUE VOICE OF ADVENTISTS

fully."[9] "Now is the time to prepare. The seal of God will never be placed upon the forehead of an impure man or woman. It will never be placed upon the forehead of the ambitious, world-loving man or woman. It will never be placed upon the forehead of men or women of false tongues or deceitful hearts. All who receive the seal of God must be without spot before God—candidates for heaven."[10]

The work of the Holy Spirit is to cooperate with everyone who chooses to develop this Christ-reflecting life, thus preparing such people to receive God's seal of approval. "The impartation of the Spirit is the impartation of the life of Christ. Those only who are thus taught of God, those only who possess the inward working of the Spirit, and in whose life the Christ-life is manifested, can stand as true representatives of the Saviour."[11]

How will those sealed regard themselves? As superior achievers? As the spiritual elite of the universe? Hardly! They will not reflect the spirit of those who, because of wrong ideas of sanctification, make "boastful claim to freedom from sin,"[12] declaring "I am sinless; I am holy."[13]

Those who come closest to Jesus "discern most clearly the frailty and sinfulness of humanity" and that "their only hope is in the merit of a crucified and risen Saviour."[14] Only those who have tasted the full heat of temptation and overcome as Jesus overcame (Revelation 3:21) will have discerned "the purity of His character" and the "exceeding sinfulness of sin."[15] At every step of their growth in grace, and never more so than when fulfilling the conditions for those who are sealed, true believers continue to sense ever more deeply their unworthiness. Only those ready to be sealed will have fully realized that the Lord is their righteousness—*all* their righteousness—and that the believers of themselves have nothing at all to offer that merits salvation. Galatians 6:14. Only those who are completely dependent upon the Holy Spirit for "grace to help in time of need" (Hebrews 4:16) will be able to "reflect the image of Jesus fully"—because Jesus demonstrated that in order to live a sinless life, each person must depend upon God completely. John 5:30. By God's grace those sealed subdue every inclination to sin, every propensity to serve self rather than do the will of God—all the while knowing that without this total dependence upon Christ's imparted grace, they would be overcome by the sophistries of evil. They have learned through experience that their "only ground of hope is in the righteousness of Christ imputed to [them], and in that wrought by His Spirit working in and through [them]."[16]

Those who are sealed trust completely in God's love and will; they have restfully entrusted their lives to His wisdom. Fully aware of how subtle and deceiving sin is, they have settled into God's truths in every aspect of their lives. Christian love is the hallmark of their reputation. They are demonstrating that love truly is the fulfilling of the law. Romans 13:10. Such self-giving relationships signal that they have reached "mature manhood, to the measure of the stature of the fullness of Christ." Ephesians 4:13. This loving outreach to a world that needs this witness to written and demonstrated truth fulfills the biblical expectations of Christian perfection. God is pleased and unembarrassed to write His name "on their foreheads." Revelation 14:1.

LATTER RAIN DELAYED

Thus, not to let the Holy Spirit complete His special work, not to permit Him to do His work of transforming selfish, greedy, vain men and women into gracious reflections of Jesus, is to delay that time when God will have a people who will fulfill His purpose in the last days.

Just as the tares among the wheat adversely affected the ripening of the harvest and "counteracted to a great degree the work of the sower, so sin among the people of God frustrates, in a measure, the plan of Jesus to save fallen man from the power of Satan and render the barren ground of the human heart fruitful of good works."[17]

The latter rain is delayed until God's people are ready for it; the latter rain will not add divine efficiency to the missionary outreach of a people who would not rightly represent the God supplying the power that could do wonders. God is jealous for His truth and will not give power to people who will embarrass the truth by their behavior: "I was shown that

THE END: THE UNIQUE VOICE OF ADVENTISTS

if God's people make no efforts on their part, but wait for the refreshing to come upon them and remove their wrongs and correct their errors: if they depend upon that to cleanse them from filthiness of the flesh and spirit, and fit them to engage in the loud cry of the third angel, they will be found wanting. The refreshing or power of God comes only on those who have prepared themselves for it by doing the work which God bids them, namely, cleansing themselves from all filthiness of the flesh and spirit, perfecting holiness in the fear of God."[18]

LOUD CRY, POWER AND GLORY

The public manifestation of the latter rain is known as the "loud cry" to the world. The world will then see and hear the result of this divine supplementation as faithful commandment keepers reach out with new fervor and credibility. The impact of this divine-human cooperation will be inescapable.[19] The worldwide effect of the loud cry will be decisions everywhere, rejecting or accepting the call of those who faithfully represent Jesus in word and life. "The love of Christ, the love of our brethren, will testify to the world that we have been with Jesus and learned of Him. Then will the message of the third angel swell to a loud cry, and the whole earth will be lightened with the glory of the Lord."[20]

John the revelator refers to the work of the loud cry as "great power" and "glory." Revelation 18:1, K.J.V. ("great authority" and "bright with his splendor," R.S.V.). Whatever reflects God's character is "glory." Christians who reflect God's glory provide sufficient evidence that God's way of life through commandment keeping is not only possible but also the answer to the great philosophical and theological questions regarding truth and love.[21] Reflecting "the glory [character] of our Lord Jesus Christ" is God's purpose for Christians, which Paul wrote to the Thessalonians about. 2 Thessalonians 2:14.[22]

We are told that the message of Revelation 18:1-6 is the loud cry of the third angel;[23] that when those who know the truth truly live it, then God will reveal His promised power and the earth will be lighted with His glory.[24]

BETWEEN NOW AND THEN

The loud cry prophecy of Revelation 18 depicts decision time for the world and for the church. Church members who have procrastinated, or who have served both God and mammon, now make their irrevocable decision either to continue their rationalizing and their normal behavior, or to commit themselves unreservedly to God, demonstrating radically new life patterns. Faithful church members make new strides in Christian witnessing. "Shining with holy consecration," they "hasten from place to place" proclaiming the message from heaven. The light of truth penetrates "everywhere, the truth is seen in its clearness, and honest children of God sever the bands which have held them."[25]

The "sealing," the "latter rain," and the "loud cry" are simultaneous events. That is, as long as people are undecided (and only God knows) the life and message of sealed people will be reaching out for them to join those who keep the commandments and the faith of Jesus. Up to the close of probationary time, the group of sealed people continues to enlarge as the latter rain and loud cry are used by God to bring people to decision.

MARK OF THE BEAST

The fearful prediction and dire consequences surrounding "the mark of the beast" (Revelation 14:9, 16:2, 19:20) are applicable when all have had the truth brought clearly to them. No one suffers the wrath of God directed against those who have the symbolic mark of the beast until the truth has been brought home in convincing ways—and rejected. A gracious God would not do otherwise. The responsibility resting upon His representatives in these final hours is great indeed as they clearly and fairly proclaim His last message of mercy: "With the issue thus clearly brought before him, whoever shall trample upon God's law to obey a human enactment receives the mark of the beast. . . . But not one is made to suffer the wrath of God's law until the truth has been brought home to his mind and conscience, and has been rejected. There are many who have never had an opportunity to hear the special truths for this time. The obligation of the fourth commandment has never been set before them in its true light. He who reads every heart and tries every motive will leave none who desire a knowledge of the truth, to be deceived as to the issue of the controversy. The decree is not to be urged upon the people blindly. Everyone is to have sufficient light to make his decision intelligently."[26]

HOSTILITY AND COERCION

Obviously, and naturally it seems, as one looks at world history, hostile reaction arises when truth cuts into established social customs and human aspirations. The work of the third angel, especially that phase described as the work of the supplementing fourth angel of Revelation 18—with the glory of God reflected in the work and life of His people—is not a time of great peace and world brotherhood. To reject truth is not a simple decision akin to choosing one's toothpaste. When one rejects the restraints of conscience, he feels no qualms about hostility and coercion against those who represent the truth that he forthrightly rejects. Examples abound, such as the religious and political leaders who finally could take no more of Jesus Christ, or Stephen, or Paul. Or the terrible anger, the hysterical frustration, of those through the centuries who have destroyed noble reputations or even tortured and killed those they could not agree with. Rejecting truth is a total response of beclouded reason and unrestrained emotion.

The strong arm of civil power will be linked to the sophisticated, but maddened influence of religious leaders. In fact, "the clergy will put forth almost superhuman efforts to shut away the light lest it should shine upon their flocks. By every means at their command they will endeavor to suppress the discussion of these vital questions."[27]

By misrepresentation and falsehood, the desperate companionship of spiritual wickedness in high places will demoralize those who, though believing the truth, have never committed their self-absorbed lives to obeying it fully. A large group of Seventh-day Adventists will repudiate their former loyalties, not willing to abandon all earthly ties that compromise a wholehearted loyalty to the commandments of God and the faith of Jesus.[28]

But many will be the ministers and people of all denominations who will join the faithful commandment keepers, including many more who saw nothing satisfying in Christianity before this clear call of God's last invitation.[29]

Great world-sweeping counter-religious movements will seem to enjoy supernatural endowments; remarkable healings coupled with apparent conversions and emotional excitement will make it appear that God Himself is especially blessing those forces opposing the worldwide call of Sabbath keepers.[30]

SPIRITUALISM

Spiritualism will play a significant role in last-day religious revivals. Those who would be easily moved and deceived by wonder-working powers, the healing of the sick, and new, exalted religious fervor, will be easy prey to Bible-quoting leaders who preach peace and safety while probation closes on them.[31]

In fact, spiritualists (and anyone who believes in the immortality of the soul will find it extremely difficult to gainsay spiritualism) and Sunday advocates will unite in their attempt to silence the commandment keepers. The periodic economic distresses, moral decadence, and other calamities will be blamed on those who resist Sunday observance; they will be called "troublers of the people."[32]

LABOR UNIONS

Joining spiritualism and Sunday advocates will be the enormous power of the labor unions. With plausible reasons that appeal to people in crisis who want immediate solutions to long-standing problems, labor unions eventually will direct oppressive power against those who do not comply with the wishes of the majority.[33]

The pressures will build, heated by the hostility of religious and political leaders who cannot directly prove the Sabbath keepers wrong and by the impatience of the majority who rarely tolerate dissent for long. In the United States, the tension reaches to legislative halls, where representatives of the people enact laws abolishing long-standing guarantees em-

THE END: THE UNIQUE VOICE OF ADVENTISTS

bedded in the American Constitution and Bill of Rights. Such action will be duplicated in all lands of the world. "The dignitaries of church and state will unite to bribe, persuade, or compel all classes to honor the Sunday. The lack of divine authority will be supplied by oppressive enactments. Political corruption is destroying love of justice and regard for truth; and even in free America, rulers and legislators, in order to secure public favor, will yield to the popular demand for a law enforcing Sunday observance. Liberty of conscience, which has cost so great a sacrifice, will no longer be respected."[34]

But Sunday agitation on the part of the labor unions, established church leaders, and others provides a dramatic setting for a wider hearing of the third angel's message as understood by Seventh-day Adventists.[35]

SUNDAY LAW

The enforcement of universal Sunday laws becomes the last act in the dramatic controversy between commandment keepers and opposing forces. Although character decides destiny and determines whether one is safe to save, the seventh-day Sabbath is the visible evidence of obedience. For this reason, "the Sabbath will be the great test of loyalty, for it is the point of truth especially controverted."[36] Eventually, the power attending the Sabbath keeper's message arouses fierce opposition; conscientious obedience is called rebellion, normal civilities are withdrawn, and civil penalties, even to the death penalty, are directed against Sabbath keepers.[37]

What is the end result of this fearful conflict? What can be expected when parent turns against child, and longtime friends disavow earlier loyalties? Truth awakens and draws "a large number" to take "their stand upon the Lord's side";[38] "a multitude not of their faith, seeing that God is with His people, will unite with them in serving the Redeemer."[39]

In this turbulent period God's restraining Spirit is totally rejected by those who place convenience, status, and lifelong habits before obedience to His commandments. This

BETWEEN NOW AND THEN

rejection of God's tempering, restraining Spirit on the conscience ushers in the seven last plagues, so dramatically described in Revelation 15 and 16. Without the controlling power of the Holy Spirit humanity is a terrible force and channel for evil.

WHO SURVIVES?

What kinds of people survive this formidable opposition, thus keeping their loyalty to God and their Christlike witness unsullied? Those who have permitted the Holy Spirit to transform their lives into a living demonstration of biblical principles. They have allowed the gospel seed to mature into a harvest of the fruit of the Spirit. Galatians 5:22, 23. They have separated sin from their lives by the grace of God. They have cooperated "with the agencies which Heaven employs in the work of conforming our characters to the divine model."[40] Although they have learned that "the more nearly the Christian imitates the divine Pattern, the more surely will he make himself a mark for the attacks of Satan,"[41] their love and loyalty to God only deepen.

Assailed with the fiercest and most subtle pressures and temptations, God's people stand unmoved. They have learned through experience that "Christ will give strength to all who seek it. No man without his own consent can be overcome by Satan. The tempter has no power to control the will or to force the soul to sin. He may distress, but he cannot contaminate. He can cause agony, but not defilement. The fact that Christ has conquered should inspire His followers with courage to fight manfully the battle against sin and Satan."[42]

How does this loyalty and character-witness relate to the closing arguments in the great controversy between God and Satan—the larger stage on which every man, woman, and child are players? Such will be our consideration in the next chapter.

THE END: THE UNIQUE VOICE OF ADVENTISTS

References

1. Ellen G. White, *The Great Controversy*, p. 594.
2. *Ibid.*, p. 598.
3. For a review of Seventh-day Adventist thinking regarding the fulfillment of Daniel 11:36-39, see *The Ministry*, March 1954; *S.D.A. Bible Commentary*, vol. 4, Comments on Daniel 11.
4. James White, *Review and Herald*, November 29, 1877.
5. "The signs which He Himself gave of His coming have been fulfilled, and by the teaching of God's word we may know that the Lord is at the door."—White, *Christ's Object Lessons*, p. 227. See also White, *Testimonies*, vol. 5, p. 711.
6. See P. Gerard Damsteegt, *Foundations*, pp. 185, 211, 212, 216, 218, 226, 235, 245-247, 252, 253, 296.
7. Ellen G. White, *Testimonies*, vol. 5, p. 214. See also White, *Early Writings*, p. 71.
8. White, *Review and Herald*, May 21, 1895. See also *The Ministry of Healing*, p. 37.
9. White, *Early Writings*, p. 71.
10. White, *Testimonies*, vol. 5, p. 216. See also pp. 213, 214.
11. White, *Gospel Workers*, p. 285. "The sanctification of the soul by the working of the Holy Spirit is the implanting of Christ's nature in humanity. Gospel religion is Christ in the life—a living, active principle. It is the grace of Christ revealed in character and wrought out in good works. The principles of the gospel cannot be disconnected with any department of practical life. Every line of Christian experience and labor is to be a representation of the life of Christ."—White, *Christ's Object Lessons*, p. 384, See also *The Desire of Ages*, p. 827.
12. White, *The Great Controversy*, p. 471.
13. White, *The Acts of the Apostles*, pp. 561, 562.
14. White, *The Great Controversy*, p. 471.
15. White, *The Acts of the Apostles*, p. 561.
16. White, *Steps to Christ*, p. 63.
17. Ellen G. White Comments, *S.D.A. Bible Commentary*, vol. 5, p. 1094.
18. White, *Testimonies*, vol. 1, p. 619. "The great outpouring of the Spirit of God, which lightens the whole earth with his glory, will not come until we have an enlightened people, that know by experience what it means to be laborers together with God. When we have entire, wholehearted consecration to the service of Christ, God will recognize the fact by an outpouring of his Spirit without measure; but this will not be while the largest portion of the church are not laborers together with God. God cannot pour out his Spirit when selfishness and self-indulgence are so manifest; when a spirit prevails that, if put into words, would express that answer of Cain,—'Am I my brother's keeper?' "—White, *Review and Herald*, July 21, 1896.
19. "With the great truth we have been privileged to receive, we should,

and under the Holy Spirit's power we could, become living channels of light. . . . The truth would be expressed by life and character, and by lips touched with the living coal from off God's altar. . . . We shall magnify the Lord, the God of all grace, who has magnified Christ. And he will reveal his power through us, making us as sharp sickles in the harvest-field."— White, *Review and Herald,* February 14, 1899.
    20. White, *Testimonies,* vol. 6, p. 401.
    21. White, *Christ's Object Lessons,* pp. 414-420.
    22. White, *The Desire of Ages,* p. 341.
    23. White, *Testimonies,* vol. 8, p. 118.
    24. White, *Testimonies,* vol. 9, p. 46.
    25. White, *The Great Controversy,* p. 612.
    26. *Ibid.,* pp. 604, 605.
    27. *Ibid.,* p. 607.
    28. *Ibid.,* p. 608. See *Testimonies,* vol. 6, pp. 400, 401.
    29. White, *Testimonies,* vol. 8, p. 41.
    30. White, *The Great Controversy,* p. 464.
    31. *Ibid.,* pp. 588, 589.
    32. *Ibid.,* pp. 587-590.
    33. White, *Selected Messages,* bk. 2, pp. 141, 142.
    34. White, *The Great Controversy,* p. 592; see also p. 581; White *Testimonies,* vol. 4, p. 451.
    35. *Ibid.,* p. 606.
    36. *Ibid.,* p. 605.
    37. *Ibid.,* pp. 590, 604, 607, 608.
    38. *Ibid.,* pp. 611, 612.
    39. Ellen G. White, *Review and Herald,* February 25, 1902.
    40. White, *The Great Controversy,* p. 623.
    41. *Ibid.,* p. 510.
    42. *Ibid.*

God's People Vindicate His Government

At the heart of the great controversy between Christ and Satan is law—God's law. From the beginning Satan's purpose has been to destroy that law. And the closing events of world history will focus on this long-standing conflict concerning the moral law of God.[1]

Why God's law? Because the moral law is the reflection of the way God is; God's law is the mirror of His character, the expression of the way life is affirmed and maintained. To defy any of God's laws is to court disaster because all acts have consequences. To go contrary to love, unselfishness, and submission to reality is to implant within the rebel a self-destruct principle whereby the seeds of rebellion eventually produce woeful results.

God is not capricious, severe, or arbitrary about His moral law any more than the spinning of the earth on its axis is an expression of selfish arrogance. Law, moral or natural, is the description of how the creation functions best. People fulfill their potential and purpose for existing when they love, defer to, and serve each other. That is the way God is, and that is the way He made his created beings.

That is why any attempts to abolish God's law, moral or natural, is an exercise in the absurd. How can anyone declare that the law of gravity is null and void; that it has served its purpose and is no longer necessary; or, that the law of gravity is arbitrary, severe, and not in anyone's best interest.

But such has been Satan's attacks on the moral law of God. He has represented God's law as a "law of selfishness,"[2] that it serves only to straitjacket the freedom and initiative of created beings, forcing submission and a phony love. He accused God of demanding obedience and love although He Himself would not unselfishly care for the needs of such "insignificant creatures as man."[3]

GOD'S PEOPLE VINDICATE HIS GOVERNMENT

Furthermore, Satan charged that "God had made a law which men could not keep,"[4] that it is impossible for men and women to obey its precepts.[5]

These indictments are profoundly serious. They charge God not to be fair or loving. How would God convince anybody that such accusations were false? By arguing the point, by speaking louder, or waving a bigger stick? No, to act in any of these ways would not have been like God. In fact, if He did, Satan's point would have been made: God is the cosmic bully; whatever He wants, He gets by intimidation. The untold billions of obeisant angels and men do not bow in adoration but cower in fear and prudence. And so Satan's charges would go on—the picture would never be clear.

But God did act—always lovingly. Always caring for the sacred precincts of reason in the soul of every created being, God put Himself on trial. We knew Him first as the baby Boy in Bethlehem, then soon as the Carpenter from Nazareth, and eventually as the Teacher sent from God. And now, as the risen Saviour, our High Priest.

All worlds were focused on this amazing drama—God becoming man, man in every sense of the word. And, forever, retaining His human nature in the heavenly courts as an everlasting pledge of the faithfulness of God.[6]

IMPRISONED WITHIN OWN CREATION

Contemplate the thought. It staggers the human mind. The Lord of Creation imprisoning Himself within His own creation. The Eternal God, who walked among the stars and whirled new universes into their orbits, to be forever cabined within time and space—this stretches the mind of men and women across unlimited oceans of love. Jesus truly gave Himself to Planet Earth and to the human race forever!

But why? Why this infinite humiliation, this self-limitation? The answer echoes throughout the universe: God loved His creation so much that there would be no limit to how far He would go to erase all doubts, all seeds of doubt, regarding the falseness of Satan's accusations.

Jesus came to this world to erase the cloud that Satan had flung up around the character of God and the fairness of His government. "By His life and His death, Christ proved that God's justice did not destroy His mercy, but that sin could be forgiven, and that the law is righteous, and can be perfectly obeyed. Satan's charges were refuted. God had given man unmistakable evidence of His love."[7]

Jesus did not come to prove that God could keep His commandments or that Adam and Eve need not have sinned; He came into this world as every child of Adam, subject to the same laws of heredity common to every newborn baby.[8] "In this earth He performed His mission and fulfilled His office; and, by obedience to the law of God, He testified to all its immutable character, while at the same time proving that its precepts could be perfectly obeyed through His grace by every son and daughter of Adam."[9]

Many were the reasons for Christ coming to this world—all of them necessary in making possible the plan of salvation. But none of those reasons is more important than His answer to Satan regarding whether the law of God could be kept by human beings, at any time, in the history of the world. "In Him was found the perfect ideal. To reveal this ideal as the only true standard for attainment; to show what every human being might become; what, through the indwelling of humanity by divinity, all who received Him would become—for this, Christ came to the world. He came to show how men are to trained as befits the sons of God; how on earth they are to practice the principles and to live the life of heaven."[10]

CANCELLED SATAN'S ACCUSATIONS

In proving that a human being, encumbered with all the liabilities of human nature,[11] could by the power of the indwelling Spirit of God obey God's laws, freely and without coercion, Jesus canceled Satan's accusation of unfairness. In fact, His example of obedience proved that the nicest, happiest, most composed person in the midst of life's great distresses was a man of faith and a commandment keeper. He proved that God will ask nothing from His

GOD'S PEOPLE VINDICATE HIS GOVERNMENT

created beings that He Himself does not do. No question about it, Jesus vindicated the fairness of God.

But in the plan of salvation was that enough? What Jesus did anchored the plan of salvation forever—it will work as promised. But was the full controversy settled by our Lord's life and death? Apparently, there was more to be done before the last doubt would be erased, before God could fairly close probationary time for men and women of Planet Earth. God was willing to risk His reputation even further—Christ's followers would be further answers to Satan's charges. In God's scheme, such a vindication would supply the indisputable evidence that God has not asked too much from His created beings when He asks for obedience; the demonstration of commandment keepers reflecting the faith of Jesus would settle forever whether love and unselfish service is the best way to find self-fulfillment and peace amidst all the options that have been tossed up for grabs throughout this long night of controversy between God and Satan.

As we have discussed in earlier chapters, the office work of the Holy Spirit is to reproduce in men and women the character of Jesus.[12] Without the Holy Spirit as a regenerating agent, "the sacrifice of Christ would have been of no avail." Christ gave the Holy Spirit "as a divine power to overcome all hereditary and cultivated tendencies to evil, and to impress His own character upon His church."[13]

This growth of the gospel seed, this fructifying of the fruit of the Spirit, this maturation of Christian character was the purpose of Christ's earthly ministry. It was His way of glorifying the Father. But the same purpose and commission was given to His followers as well: "As thou didst send me into the world, so I have sent them into the world. . . . I in them and thou in me, . . . that the world may know that thou hast sent me." John 17:18, 23.

We are told: "The Saviour came to glorify the Father by the demonstration of His love; so the Spirit was to glorify Christ by revealing His grace to the world. The very image of God is to be reproduced in humanity. The honor of God, the honor of Christ, is involved in the perfection of the character of His people."[14]

THE END: THE UNIQUE VOICE OF ADVENTISTS

Even though Satan's disguise was torn away at the cross—his lying, hateful, heart exposed to the universe—there were still some lingering questions in the minds of unfallen beings. Apparently Calvary did not clear up "all that was involved in the great controversy." God knew that more time and a broader, perhaps more risky demonstration was yet needed so that "the principles at stake" would be "more fully revealed."[15]

ANOTHER DEMONSTRATION

Such a demonstration will be on full display in the last generation of Christians who truly "keep the commandments of God and the faith of Jesus." Revelation 14:12. Then Paul's picture will be complete when men and women "live for the praise of his glory," fulfilling "the purpose of his will, to the praise of his glorious grace." Ephesians 1:12, 5, 6.

Since 1844 a special urgency has rested upon those who perceive their destiny as human instruments for proclaiming the three messages of Revelation 14. Such people, to fulfill their task, must be the people for whom God waits to vindicate His character and government. The doctrine of the sanctuary, in particular, becomes involved in explaining how the development of such a people is an integral part of the plan of salvation.[16]

One of the central themes of the sanctuary doctrine is that the sanctuary in heaven is finally cleansed, prior to the close of probationary time, when God's people on earth are cleansed from sinful thoughts and acts.[17] Such has been the emphasis of many Adventist scholars through the years.

One of the most urgent messages of the sanctuary doctrine since 1844 is that something special is required of God's followers in terms of character development that may not have been so crucial to the development of the church heretofore. For two reasons: (1) When God's people attain the quality of character described in Revelation 14:12, for which He was given every needed divine power to achieve, then Jesus' work as High Priest is finished. (2) When such a people are cleansed from sin and reflect the image of Jesus winsomely and courageously, then God's honor is vindi-

GOD'S PEOPLE VINDICATE HIS GOVERNMENT

cated, His government cleared of Satan's accusations.[18]

The ripening of the gospel harvest, the reflection of Christ's character in His obedient people, is the irrefutable argument that God's law has not been unfair, that God has offered to us freedom and love when He asked for our obedience. So, "the honor of Christ must stand complete in the perfection of the character of His chosen people."[19]

WHY JESUS WAITS

Therefore Jesus will wait for this vindication of His name in His commandment keeping people. The missionary impulse of the church will slumber until such people understand their role in the plan of salvation.

God never decreed that time should last into the late twentieth century. He longs to pour out the latter rain on those who have cleansed "the soul temple of every defilement."[20] He longs for His people to be so settled into the truth,[21] so comfortable with His way of life, that He can impart His seal of approval and point to them without embarrassment in a worldwide mission appeal: "Here they are, here are my people who keep my commandments and have 'the faith of Jesus.'"

Such people prove Satan a liar! Even as Jesus showed the way. God has not asked the impossible. Much to the contrary, God's faithful in the last generation prove that the gospel is God's way out of the quicksand of sin and all its consequences. They reflect the life witness of Enoch, Daniel, and all the others in times past who became overcomers, and thus the vindicators of the wisdom, justice, and love of God. Job's experience will be reproduced: "According to his faith, so was it unto Job. 'When He hath tried me,' he said, 'I shall come forth as gold.' Job 23:10. So it came to pass. By his patient endurance he vindicated his own character, and thus the character of Him whose representative he was."[22]

Such is the urgency resting on those who claim to be commandment keepers and heralds of a soon-coming Saviour. "If there was ever a people in need of constantly increasing light from heaven, it is the people that, in this time

THE END: THE UNIQUE VOICE OF ADVENTISTS

of peril, God has called to be the depositaries of His holy law and to vindicate His character before the world."[23]

Here is a people who prove that all these lofty statements about the promises of God and His power in behalf of His people, are more than theological statements. They are living examples of the good news—that the evil one has been vanquished, that forgiveness is a dynamic experience, that sins can be overcome, that sinners can be overcomers! Such is the good news that honest, weary, struggling men and women truly want to know. Sincere voices ask, "Is the battle worth it? In fact, is there such a thing as victory?" Although they have read that Jesus was obedient, and that His immediate followers have written Yes in their letters to the Christian church, the living witness of advent-oriented commandment keepers in the last days will be the crowning evidence that the Bible means what it says when it expresses, in so many ways, that God indeed "is able to keep you from falling." Jude 24.

Such people have fulfilled God's purpose for waiting. They have accomplished their role in the plan of salvation: "The Lord desires through His people to answer Satan's charges by showing the result of obedience to right principles."[24] How Seventh-day Adventists relate to this role and understand their mission and message will be the theme of our next and final chapter.

References

    1. Ellen G. White, *The Great Controversy*, p. 582.
    2. White, *The Desire of Ages*, p. 24.
    3. White, *Signs of the Times*, January 20, 1890.
    4. White, *The Faith I Live By* (Washington, D.C.: Review and Herald Publishing Association, 1958), p. 114; see White, *Christ's Object Lessons*, p. 314.
    5. White, *The Desire of Ages*, p. 24. Many forms of attacking the law of God exist, even within the Christian church. They are all forms of antinomianism (against, or instead of, law). Such attacks include the following arguments: the moral law was abolished at the cross; Jesus kept the law for us—His holy character is imputed to the saints because it is impossible for men and women to keep the law, even with the help of the Holy Spirit; there is no immutable law because, in the nature of human

GOD'S PEOPLE VINDICATE HIS GOVERNMENT

development, truth is progressive; and any concept derived from the doctrine of predestination where some are elected to receive faith and some not, or where faith is considered more of an intellectual assent, a recognition of a total redemption provided as a gift without human cooperation required in any phase of the redemptive process.

6. *Ibid.,* p. 25.
7. *Ibid.,* p. 762.
8. Ellen G. White, Manuscript 1, 1892, reprinted in *Review and Herald,* June 17, 1976; see also *The Desire of Ages,* p. 49.
9. White, *Bible Echo,* vol. 10, No. 22, p. 172. See also *The Desire of Ages,* pp. 24, 49, 664; *Signs of the Times,* July 18, 1892.
10. White, *Education,* pp. 73, 74. "The great Teacher came into our world not only to atone for sin, but to be a teacher both by precept and example. He came to show man how to keep the law in humanity, so that man might have no excuse for following his own defective judgment. We see Christ's obedience. His life without sin. His lifelong obedience is a reproach to disobedient humanity. The obedience of Christ is not to be put aside as altogether different to the obedience he requires of us individually. Christ has shown us that it is possible for all humanity to obey the laws of God. He served as a son with the Father. Just so we must every one serve with God, not in our own improvised plans. Serving is a living service when self is not made supreme. . . .

"Our Saviour took up the true relationship of a human being as the son of God. We are sons and daughters of God. In order to know how to behave ourselves circumspectly, we must follow where Christ leads the way. For thirty years he lived the life of a perfect man, meeting the highest standard of perfection. Then let man, however imperfect, hope in God, saying not, If I were of a different disposition I would serve God, but bring himself to Him in true service. Christ has invited you to do this."—White, Letter 69, 1897, pp. 10, 11.

"This lamentable condition would have known no change or hope if Jesus had not come down to our world to be man's Saviour and Example. In the midst of a world's moral degradation he stands, a beautiful and spotless character, the one model for man's imitation."—White, *Signs of the Times,* December 22, 1887.

"Jesus came down from Heaven to teach us how to live; and his life was one of toil and self-denial. He went about doing good, and those who are truly his representatives will follow his example in working for the good of others."—White, *Signs of the Times,* April 21, 1887.

11. White, *The Desire of Ages,* p. 117.
12. See chapter eight of this book.
13. White, *The Desire of Ages,* p. 671.
14. *Ibid.*
15. *Ibid.,* p. 761.
16. See the author's *Why Jesus Waits* (Washington D.C.: Review and Herald Publishing Association, 1976).
17. For example: Stephen N. Haskell, "The Sanctuary Question From

the Standpoint of the book of Hebrews," *Review and Herald,* August 13, 1901; W. W. Prescott, "Studies in the Gospel Message, *Review and Herald,* July 15, 1902; "The Gospel Message For Today," *General Conference Bulletin,* April 2, 1903; E. G. White, sermon delivered October 20, 1888, reprinted in A. V. Olson, *Through Crisis to Victory,* p. 267.

18. See Mervyn Maxwell, "Ready For His Appearing," an essay in Douglass, et al, *Perfection* (Nashville, Tenn.: Southern Publishing Association, 1975).
19. Ellen G. White, *Signs of the Times,* November 25, 1897.
20. White, *Testimonies,* vol. 5, p. 214.
21. Ellen G. White Comments on Ezekiel 9:2-4, *S.D.A. Bible Commentary,* vol. 4, p. 1161.
22. White, *Education,* p. 156.
23. White, *Testimonies,* vol. 5, p. 746.
24. White, *Testimonies,* vol. 6, p. 11.

Adventism's Highest Priority

In essence, this chapter is a summary. But a summary with purpose and application. We have discovered that Jesus has been waiting to return for over a century, that He is waiting for a prepared people, a people who demonstrate the fruition of the gospel seed, a demonstration that proves Satan wrong and God right about sin and righteousness.

The questions are: *Who* knows all this and if it is so important, how will the world ever know? If every other voice proclaiming an imminent return of Jesus, basing their evidence on such current events as the return of the Jews to Palestine and the rise of Russia as the king of the north, is wrong in their biblical interpretation, then an awesome responsibility rests upon those *who* know why Jesus continues to wait. If men and women, the world over, Christians or not, deplore the moral decadence of the times and fear the potential catastrophes built into the modern technological world—who will give them a word of hope they can trust without fear of a credibility gap? For those equally bright men and women who see nothing but solutions and breakthroughs in the future, who will temper their optimism with the reality of impending judgment?

With a deep sense of insufficiency—trembling with respect for the honest-hearted representing all churches, movements, and religions—Seventh-day Adventists reach out to all, presenting the truth as it is in Jesus. No sweeping denunciations come from Adventist tongues or pens. No arrogant claims. Only the promises of Jesus must come from their lips. God forbid that anything but love and humility should motivate each invitation to listen to what Adventists believe to be God's last call to a judgment-bound world.

Seventh-day Adventists understand their mission in terms of a twin purpose issuing from a double emphasis: To prepare a people to meet the Lord and to alert a world with a judgment-hour message. On many occasions, these biblical concepts (Ephesians 3:9-11; Titus 2:13, 14; 2 Peter 3:11-14; 1 John 3:2, 3; Revelation 14:12) are reiterated by Ellen White:

"It is God's purpose to manifest through His people the principles of His kingdom. That in life and character they may reveal these principles, He desires to separate them from the customs, habits, and practices of the world. . . . By beholding the goodness, the mercy, the justice, and the love of God revealed in His church, the world is to have a representation of His character. And when the law of God is thus exemplified in the life, even the world will recognize the superiority of those who love and fear and serve God above every other people in the world. . . . It is His purpose that by exemplifying the truth in their lives they shall be a praise in the earth. The grace of Christ is sufficient to bring this about."[1]

"In a special sense Seventh-day Adventists have been set in this world as watchmen and light bearers. To them has been entrusted the last message of mercy for a perishing world. On them is shining wonderful light from the Word of God. What manner of persons, then, ought they to be? . . . Heavenly angels have long been waiting for human agents . . . to cooperate with them in the great work to be done."[2]

A CREDIBLE HEARING

Although both emphases are crucial and equally essential, for maximum effectiveness and in point of time, one must precede the other: Character preparation of God's professed people will precede a credible hearing, wherein men and women truly hear the gospel and thus are able to make an enlightened decision either to accept or reject.

Seventh-day Adventists must be awake to their destiny before they can consummate it. Their first order of business is to clarify their mission to themselves—before the world can be convinced regarding their message.

Understanding Adventism's highest priority involves a clear understanding of what God is trying to do about sin here and now and how He plans to use "those who keep the commandments of God and the faith of Jesus" (Revelation 14:12) as an integral part of the "good news" that must go to all the world. With the understanding must come a commitment, so that such truths will be translated into habit patterns, etched ever deeper by the Holy Spirit in daily cooperation with the committed Christian.

Ellen White has appealed time and again: "The world today is in crying need of a revelation of Christ Jesus in the person of His saints. God desires that His people shall stand before the world a holy people. Why?—because there is a world to be saved by the light of gospel truth; and as the message of truth that is to call men out of darkness into God's marvelous light is given by the church, the lives of its members, sanctified by the Spirit of truth, are to bear witness to the verity of the messages proclaimed."[3]

The call is specific, clear, and reasonable: "We should daily obtain a deep and living experience in the work of perfecting Christian character. We should daily receive the holy oil, that we may impart to others. . . . We are to praise God; to show forth His glory in a righteous character. . . . We are nearing the Judgment, and those who bear the message of warning to the world must have clean hands and pure hearts."[4]

Peter's admonition will be fulfilled and God's purpose achieved: "Maintain good conduct among the Gentiles . . . that they may see your good deeds and glorify God on the day of visitation." 1 Peter 2:12. The destiny of a people who "keep the commandments of God and the faith of Jesus" will be accomplished: "The great, grand work of bringing out a people who will have Christlike characters, and who will be able to stand in the day of the Lord, is to be accomplished."[5]

MORE THAN SAVING ONE'S SOUL

There is more to being a Seventh-day Adventist than saving one's own soul. Polishing up one's own piety, as an end in itself, is a fatal misunderstanding of Christianity in general, and the mission of the Seventh-day Adventist Church in particular. Ellen White is emphatic: "Today the remant people of God are to glorify His name by proclaiming the last message of warning, the last invitation to the marriage supper of the Lamb. The only way in which they can fulfill God's expectations is by being representatives of the truth for this time.... Not with tame, lifeless utterance is the message to be given, but with clear, decided, stirring utterances. Hundreds are waiting for the warning to escape for their lives. The world needs to see in Christians an evidence of the power of Christianity."[6]

There is more to being a Seventh-day Adventist institution—school, hospital, publishing house, book center, restaurant, nursing home, or food factory—than to service the church's needs, and supply employment for Seventh-day Adventists. In many ways we have been told, "Our sanitariums are to be established for one object—the proclamation of the truth for this time. And they are to be so conducted that a decided impression in favor of the truth will be made on the minds of those who come to them for treatment."[7]

Regarding publishing houses (and the counsel applies to every Adventist institution) we have been challenged: "We are not only to publish the theory of the truth, but to present a practical illustration of it in character and life. Our publishing institutions are to stand before the world as an embodiment of Christian principles.... And all that is done in every line is to bear the impress of heaven, to show forth the excellence of the character of God.

"God has ordained that His work shall be presented to the world in distinct, holy lines. He desires His people to show by their lives the advantage of Christianity over worldiness. By His grace every provision has been made for us in all our transaction of business to demonstrate the superiority of heaven's principles over the principles of the world....

"In all our work, even in mechanical lines, God desires that the perfection of His character shall appear. The exactness, skill, tact, wisdom, and perfection which He required in the building of the earthly tabernacle, He desires to have brought into everything that shall be done in His service....

"Our institutions will give character to the work of God just according to the consecrated devotion of the workers—

ADVENTISM'S HIGHEST PRIORITY

by revealing the power of the grace of Christ to transform the life. We are to be distinguished from the world because God has placed His seal upon us, because He manifests in us His own character of love."[8]

ISSUE IS LAW AND GRACE

In other words, personally and institutionally, Adventism's highest priority is to reveal to the world, dark with misapprehension, the glory of God's character, and thus to vindicate His government. The issue is fundamentally—law and grace. Whether obedience to God's law—His way of life—is possible to be lived and produces what He has said it would. Whether God's grace—His power to transform sinners is able to make weak, self-oriented followers into reflections of His own character.

God's law will be vindicated by a people who take God's call seriously. "Our duty to obey this law is to be the burden of this last message of mercy to the world. God's law is not a new thing. It is not holiness created, but holiness made known. It is a code of principles expressing mercy, goodness, and love. It presents to fallen humanity the character of God, and states plainly the whole duty of man."[9]

God chooses to wait for this people that will prove for all time to come that His law is the code of liberty, the source of the universe's security. "God has waited long, and He is waiting still, to have the beings that are his by both creation and redemption, listen to his voice, and obey him as loving, submissive children, whose desire is to be near his side, and to have the light of his countenance shining upon them. . . . We are to have the truth planted in the heart, and teach it to others as it is in Jesus. . . . Satan and his angels are continually plotting to make void the law of God, and thus to enslave the souls of men in the toils of sin."[10]

But equally important, God is jealous for the power of His grace. This provision has always been freely offered to men and women. But along with His law, Satan has also been attacking God's grace. How confused the Christian church has been in interpreting the grace of God!

Paul commented, "He destined us in love to be his sons

THE END: THE UNIQUE VOICE OF ADVENTISTS

through Jesus Christ, according to the purpose of his will, to the praise of his glorious grace which he freely bestowed on us in the Beloved." Ephesians 1:5, 6. He urged Christians to claim this grace: "Let us then with confidence draw near to the throne of grace, that we may receive mercy and find grace to help in time of need." Hebrews 4:16.

In those who "keep the commandments of God and the faith of Jesus" (Revelation 14:12), grace has reached its purpose. Such people can truly witness to the power and wonder of God's grace: "The message of the renewing power of God's grace will be carried to every country and clime, until the truth shall belt the world."[11]

GOD'S INSTRUMENT

In 1900, Ellen White released a chapter entitled, "God's Purpose in the Church," which seems to sum up the role for Seventh-day Adventists as they function as God's instrument in the last days. In this chapter, we learn:

"It is God's purpose to manifest through His people the principles of His kingdom. That in life and character they may reveal these principles, He desires to separate them from the customs, habits, and practices of the world. . . .

"Satan is constantly urging men to accept His principles. . . . He is an accuser of the brethren, and his accusing power he is constantly using against those who work righteousness. The Lord desires through His people to answer Satan's charges by showing the result of obedience to right principles.

"All the light of the past, all the light which shines in the present and reaches forth into the future, as revealed in the word of God, is for every soul who will receive it. The glory of this light, which is the very glory of the character of Christ, is to be manifested in the individual Christian, in the family, in the church, in the ministry of the word, and in every institution established by God's people. All these the Lord designs shall be symbols of what can be done for the world. They are to be types of the saving power of truths of the gospel. They are agencies in the fulfillment of God's great purpose for the human race. . . . They are to become channels through which divine instrumentalities communicate to the world the tide of God's love. . . .

"By beholding the goodness, the mercy, the justice, and the love of God revealed in the church, the world is to have a representation of His character. And when the law of God is thus exemplified in the life, even the world will recognize the superiority of those who love and fear and serve God above every other people on the earth. . . . It is His purpose that those who practice His holy precepts shall be a distinguished people. . . .

"Not to this world only but to the universe are we to make manifest the principles of His kingdom."[12]

These are heavy words for Seventh-day Adventists as well as for their friends in other persuasions. Some Adventists believe such admonition is arrogant, perhaps misguided. Others suggest that it rests on erroneous theology—believing that Christians will always be sinners, this side of the resurrection. But Ellen White is not running past her biblical parameters. She remains this world's clearest expositor of what the Bible writers meant, and still mean, for Christians today. One of the distinguishing features of Christianity is that its members may cease to sin, may overcome all inherited and cultivated tendencies to sin.[13] The message is biblically clear: God will have a people who will cooperate with Him in overcoming all sin before the world's door is shut in the close of probationary time.[14]

The words are heavy because many generations of Adventists have not fulfilled their destiny. No profit accrues from condemning the past, especially when the present generation seems willing to pass its privileges and opportunities over to another yet unborn.

The words are heavy because Seventh-day Adventists will require more forgiveness and grace than any other people, if they are to fulfill their destiny. Total commitment in the "obedience of faith" has never been easy because we all tend to seek easier ways to get the work of God done.

The words are heavy because Adventists can easily be misunderstood. In the interests of modesty, we shy away from making what may seem to be self-serving statements.

THE END: THE UNIQUE VOICE OF ADVENTISTS

But the simple fact remains: God has always had a special people for those special times when He wanted to say something extremely important to all His children of Planet Earth. For Seventh-day Adventists that time is now.

THE COUNTY FAIR

Many years ago now, I belonged to the 4-H Club in East Longmeadow, Massachusetts. I loved to work the family garden. Every year we seemed to enlarge it further, relentlessly pushing back the forest for more potatoes and beans. Part of our challenge as 4-H members was to strive for a weedless garden—and we learned by experience that such was possible. But the goal for which all our efforts were bent was the county fair.

At the fair were long shelves of canned vegetables and fruit. Fresh vegetables and fruit were piled into baskets. Up and down the aisles went the judges passing out their blue, red, and yellow ribbons. Those tables held the best we could produce; the heaped-up quality could not be denied. No one had to argue about their quality. No one had to convince anyone that quality was there, any more than anyone has to convince another that the sun exists on a bright sunny afternoon.

For the world, it is "fair" time. Apparently Ellen White was very much acquainted with county fairs, for she wrote: "When the farmers seek to recommend or exhibit their products, they do not gather up the poorest but the best specimens. [Then she gives many examples.] . . . And why should not Christians living in these last days reveal the most attractive fruit in unselfish actions? Why should not the fruit of the commandment-keeping people of God appear in the very best representation of good works? Their words, their deportment, their dress should bear fruit of the very best quality."[15]

But apricots, beans, and squash are not grown overnight. Neither are quality Christians who have learned that commandment keeping and developing the faith of Jesus take time. Becoming a prepared person, a member of a prepared people, a person who reflects the character of God, is more than raising hands in public commitment after a compelling sermon. It is more than perfect attendance at church for 35 years, or years of teaching Christian doctrines, or healing the sick, or anything else short of growth in grace and in attaining "mature manhood, to the measure of the stature of the fullness of Christ." Ephesians 4:13.

After October 22, 1844, early Adventists reexamined the biblical prophecies, clarified the nature of the events then taking place, and thus explained the "Great Disappointment." They recognized that instead of coming to earth to cleanse it in judgment, Jesus had begun the last phase of His high priestly role in the heavenly sanctuary. As time went by, their chief concern, as they understood it, was to warn men and women of the judgment hour and that Jesus was soon to return.

But God had something further to teach His people and, through them, all honest seekers of truth everywhere. What he has tried to teach has been only slowly grasped by His people. This is not because it is difficult, but because it is the doctrine Satan fears and hates most,[16] and most troublesome for casual Christians to accept.

The reason why Jesus did not come after 1844—during the generation that saw the great signs in the sun, moon, and stars—was that His "people were not ready to meet their Lord. There was still a work of preparation to be accomplished for them. Light was to be given, directing their minds to the temple of God in heaven; and as they should by faith follow their High Priest in His administration there, new duties would be revealed. Another message of warning and instruction was to be given to the church."[17]

A SPECIAL MESSAGE TO THE CHURCH

What could be this new warning and instruction to be given, *not to the world, but to the church?* To answer this question, Ellen White unfolded the deepening significance of the sanctuary doctrine: "Those who are living upon the earth when the intercession of Christ shall cease in the sanctuary above are to stand in the sight of a holy God without a mediator. Their robes must be spotless, their characters must be purified from sin by the blood of sprinkling. Through the grace of God and their own diligent effort they must be conquerors in the battle with evil. While the investigative judgment is going forward in heaven, while the sins of penitent believers are being removed from the sanctuary, there is to be *a special work of purification,* of putting away of sin, *among God's people upon earth.* This work is more clearly presented in the messages of Revelation 14.

"When this work shall have been accomplished, the followers of Christ will be ready for His appearing."[18]

Here again, in the doctrine of the sanctuary, we have a biblical line of argument requiring a prepared people before God's work on earth is accomplished. Such overcoming, victorious Christians drive Satan to wrath and frustration (Revelation 12:17). Such people prove Satan wrong and God right—that God has not asked too much of His children when He asks and expects obedience; they settle once and for all that God's grace is stronger than years of self-absorbing, self-indulging habits, that God is worth His creation's love, respect, and loyalty.

For these reasons "Satan invents unnumbered schemes to occupy our minds, that they may not dwell upon the very work with which we ought to be best acquainted. The archdeceiver hates the great truths that bring to view an atoning sacrifice and an all-powerful mediator. He knows that with him everything depends on his diverting minds from Jesus and His truth. . . .

"Through defects in the character, Satan works to gain control of the whole mind, and he knows that if these defects are cherished, he will succeed. Therefore he is constantly seeking to deceive the followers of Christ with his fatal sophistry that it is impossible for them to overcome."[19]

The "message of warning and instruction" that the Adventist Church needed to understand, corrected and clarified what the Christian church for centuries had seen only dimly: that God is serious about sin, that He wants to save His people from its penalty and power, and that He will have a people demonstrating once and for all that His grace is more than sufficient to eradicate sin from human practice.

ADVENTISM'S HIGHEST PRIORITY

This special instruction has been known for over a century as the Laodicean message. Especially applied to Adventists who tended to regard their doctrinal clarity and remarkable missionary accomplishments as signs of God's special favor, this "counsel of the True Witness" regarded such satisfaction as "wretched" blindness and nakedness. But with the condemnation came the promise. If those who knew the truth would open their hearts to the undivided presence of the Holy Spirit, they too would be conquerors even as Jesus Himself conquered. See Revelation 3:14-21.

But merely accepting the reproof and agreeing with the high destiny promised was not yet enough. To accomplish such high purposes takes time. Ellen White saw the problem: "I saw that this message would not accomplish its work in a few short months. . . . If the counsel of the True Witness had been fully heeded, God would have wrought for His people in greater power. . . .

"If the message had been of as short duration as many of us supposed, there would have been no time for them to develop character. Many moved from feeling, not from principle and faith, and this solemn, fearful message stirred them. It wrought upon their feelings, and excited their fears, but did not accomplish the work which God designed that it should."[20]

Whatever line of thought we follow, the focus is the same: Jesus waits, waits for a prepared people, a people who have overcome even as He overcame. Adventism's highest priority is to bring their performance up to their knowledge, by the grace of God. Not in panic, but out of a sober sense of reality. For their own sense of integrity as well as out of a deepening sense of responsibility and love for their fellowmen.

Adventists alone (and may this self-awareness make them more humble and gracious with their non-Adventist friends) have an "understanding of the times, to know what Israel ought to do." 1 Chronicles 12:32. They know that their world ministry in little more than a century has required much sacrifice, and much perseverance. The results, by any standard, have been phenomenal. They have been admired even by opponents, often applauded. But to finish their task will require far more sacrifice and perseverance than they have yet dreamed.

Although Adventists generally have earned the respect of their contemporaries, probably every Adventist knows some hardship, some parting of the ways, some burden borne for Jesus that has cost some earthly friend, some once-cherished ambition.

But the questions the Lord asked Jeremiah apply with devastating frankness to every Seventh-day Adventist today: " 'If you have raced with men on foot, and they have wearied you, how will you compete with horses? And if in a safe land you fall down, how will you do in the jungle of the Jordan?' " Jeremiah 12:5.

Adventists know that someday the Jordan will swell, the easy paths will suddenly become treacherous with foes unseen, the wind will become brisk, the hill steeper. The past will not provide all the answers. What should they do?

A young man who worked for Lord Joseph Duveen suggests an answer. "Duveen, American head of the art firm that bore his name, planned in 1915 to send one of his experts to England to examine some ancient pottery. He booked passage on the *Lusitania*. The the German Embassy issued a warning that the liner might be torpedoed. Duveen wanted to call off the trip: 'I can't take the risk of your being killed,' he said to his young expert.

" 'Don't worry,' the man replied. 'I'm a strong swimmer, and when I read what was happening in the Atlantic, I began hardening myself by spending time every day in a tub of ice water. At first I could stand it only a few minutes, but this morning I stayed in that tub nearly two hours.'

"Naturally, Duveen laughed. It sounded preposterous. But this expert sailed; the *Lusitania* was torpedoed. The young man was rescued after nearly five hours in the chilly ocean, still in excellent condition."[21]

Just as this young man prepared for the probable future, so must Seventh-day Adventists, for themselves as well as for others. Adventists now must learn how to keep their eyes on Jesus in a daily companionship, conditioning themselves now under the daily guidance of the Holy Spirit, finding easy

ADVENTISM'S HIGHEST PRIORITY

victories in preparation for the tough times. All that they now mentally affirm, in times of ease, regarding disciplined living; fervent Bible study; gracious outreach to others; and firm, clearheaded resistance to evil wherever found must become a daily fact. Not a "someday" option. Not a lifestyle to be pursued only when they "see events shaping up."

Here are men and women who have permitted their Lord to bury their moral failures "into the depths of the sea." Micah 7:19. Here are those who have heard their Lord call them sons and daughters (Luke 15), heard His appeal: "Cast away from you all the transgressions which you have committed against me, and get yourselves a new heart and a new spirit!" Ezekiel 18:31.

They have learned in sunshine and shadow that God never turns His face from His children, that He can be trusted, that His blessings of peace are new every morning, fresh every evening. They have felt His everlasting arms around them when they strayed, they know the touch of the Hand outstretched to save, the throb of the Heart that beats for their salvation.

They know from experience that God can be trusted, that worshiping Him, trusting Him, and leaning on His promises lead to Paul's effusive witness: "And my God will supply every need of yours according to his riches in glory in Christ Jesus." Philippians 4:19.

Such people know that daily contemplation of Jesus Christ through Bible study and prayer, listening and submitting to the guidance of the Holy Spirit, and personal Christian witness are the only ways God's will can be known and His work of transforming their characters accomplished. They have settled forever that God means what He says about forgiving the past—all of it. About empowering them for the present—all of it. And about providing light and hope for the future—all of it. They know that God does not plan on rescuing His people with divine helicopters when the awesome troubles of the last days come. They know from divine revelation as well as sanctified common sense that God is offering battle training now so that we can endure later.

The five foolish bridesmaids (Matthew 25) expected special deliverance from their predicament, such as others had been supplying them in earlier times. But they learned too late that even God can not supply courage, trust, integrity, endurance, or moral toughness when the crisis comes. Such qualities are products of a spiritual mind-set, developed over the months and years, in cooperation with the teaching and empowering ministry of the Holy Spirit.

Character cannot be transferred. Not from husband to wife. Not from parent to child. Not from God even to His followers. In the time of crisis, character is revealed, not created.

Character deficiencies are not made up for after death or after translation. Subtle, pervasive and dangerous is the concept that God knows that depraved human beings cannot keep His law, even with the help of the Holy Spirit; that human beings can never truly be overcomers and live without committing sin. For them Jesus was not an Example for all men and women, demonstrating that it is possible to experience fierce temptation from within and without, yet without sinning. Consequently, knowing that the redeemed must have "the holiness without which no one will see the Lord" (Hebrews 12:14), such unscriptural concepts lead one to believe that a purified character will be given to the redeemed at, what some call, glorification when Jesus returns.

This teaching is dangerous because it lulls Christians to sleep. Rarely does one reach higher than the standard he sets for himself. The five foolish bridesmaids discovered this error too late. Character is not transferable; it cannot be given as a gift. Disobedience can be forgiven and such pardon is a gift; but obedience, holiness, and Christlikeness are developed—not a fact declared to be so, when it is not. "Christ has given us no assurance that to attain perfection of character is an easy matter. A noble, all-round character is not inherited. It does not come to us by accident. A noble character is earned by individual effort through the merits and grace of Christ. God gives the talents, the powers of the mind; we form the character. It is formed by hard, stern battles with self. Conflict after conflict must be waged

ADVENTISM'S HIGHEST PRIORITY

against hereditary tendencies. We shall have to criticize ourselves closely, and allow not one unfavorable trait to remain uncorrected."[22]

Sin, the rebel posture against God's law, is not inevitable or necessary in God's universe. God's people will have proven that, especially in the last generation. Paul's plea to the church will be finally taken seriously: "But fornication and all impurity or covetousness must not even be named among you, as is fitting among saints. Let there be no filthiness, nor silly talk, nor levity, which are not fitting; but instead let there be thanksgiving. Be sure of this, that no fornicator or impure man, or one who is covetous (that is an idolater), has any inheritance in the kingdom of Christ and of God. Let no one deceive you with empty words, for it is because of these things that the wrath of God comes upon the sons of disobedience." Ephesians 5:3-6.

"Put to death therefore what is earthly in you: fornication, impurity, passion, evil desire, and covetousness, which is idolatry. On account of these the wrath of God is coming. In these you once walked, when you lived in them. But now put them all away: anger, wrath, malice, slander, and foul talk from your mouth. Do not lie to one another, seeing that you have put off the old nature with its practices and have put on the new nature, which is being renewed in knowledge after the image of its creator. . . . Put on then, as God's chosen ones, holy and beloved, compassion, kindness, lowliness, meekness, and patience, forbearing one another and, if one has a complaint against another, forgiving each other; as the Lord has forgiven you, so you also must forgive. And above all these put on love, which binds everything together in perfect harmony." Colossians 3:5-14.

God's expectations for His people are not merely lofty guides, such as the North Star to the traveler—always there but beyond our grasp. "His law is a transcript of His own character, and it is the standard of all character. This infinite standard is presented to all that there may be no mistake in regard to the kind of people whom God will have to compose His kingdom. The life of Christ on earth was a perfect expression of God's law, and when those who claim to be children of God become Christlike in character, they will be obedient to God's commandments. Then the Lord can trust them to be of the number who shall compose the family of heaven. . . . They have a right to join the blood-washed throng."[23]

The conclusion of the whole matter, the point where all discussion regarding *time* in the process of sanctification ends, the central issue that every honest seeker for truth in the last days finally must face is this: God will not change the character after one dies or when Jesus comes.[24] He will not change a person who has not overcome (let us say) his tendency to a hasty temper in the days of his probationary time. Such a possibility lies outside the general approach God has taken to sin since its inception. It contradicts the biblical promises to *the overcomer* who shall "not be hurt by the second death" (Revelation 2:11); "shall be clad thus in white garments, and I will not blot his name out of the book of life" (Revelation 3:5); shall be made "a pillar in the temple of my God; never shall he go out of it, and I will write on him the name of my God" (Revelation 3:12); and shall "sit with me on my throne, as I myself conquered and sat down with my Father on his throne" (Revelation 3:21).

To wait for a change of character *after* one dies or is translated is perhaps the most subtle, and deadliest insinuations of the master deceiver. Ellen White said: "When he comes he is not to cleanse us of our sins, to remove from us the defects in our characters, or to cure us of the infirmities of our tempers and dispositions. If wrought for us at all, this work will all be accomplished before that time. When the Lord comes, those who are holy will be holy still. Those who have preserved their bodies and spirits in holiness, in sanctification and honor, will then receive the finishing touch of immortality. But those who are unjust, unsanctified, and filthy will remain so forever. No work will then be done for them to remove their defects and give them holy characters. The Refiner does not then sit to pursue His refining process and remove their sins and their corruption. This is all to be done in these hours of probation. It is *now* that this work is to be accomplished for us.

ADVENTISM'S HIGHEST PRIORITY

"We embrace the truth of God with our different faculties, and as we come under the influence of that truth, it will accomplish the work for us which is necessary to give us a moral fitness for the kingdom of glory and for the society of the heavenly angels. We are now in God's workshop. Many of us are rough stones from the quarry. But as we lay hold upon the truth of God, its influence affects us. It elevates us and removes from us every imperfection and sin, of whatever nature. Thus we are prepared to see the King in His beauty and finally to unite with the pure and heavenly angels in the kingdom of glory. It is here that this work is to be accomplished for us, here that our bodies and spirits are to be fitted for immortality.

"We are in a world that is opposed to righteousness and purity of character, and to a growth in grace. Wherever we look we see corruption and defilement, deformity and sin. And what is the work that we are to undertake here just previous to receiving immortality? It is to preserve our bodies holy, our spirits pure, that we may stand forth unstained amid the corruptions teeming around us in these last days. And if this work is accomplished we need to engage in it at once, heartily and understandingly. Selfishness should not come in here to influence us. The Spirit of God should have perfect control of us, influencing us in all our actions."[25]

Character cannot prevent troubles. Faith cannot stop the river from rising. Wise Seventh-day Adventists prudently prepare for hard times so that they will not be shaken by them. Seventh-day Adventists know that God's kingdom will triumph but only after the most hellish demonstration of frustration, selfishness, and spiteful coercion this world has ever known. Every Christian in the last days will eventually have to run with horses and manage the raging of the Jordan. Only the prepared survive. Only the prepared have the spiritual muscle that demonstrates the point that God has been making over the centuries: "Love is strong as death. . . . Many waters cannot quench love, neither can floods drown it." Song of Solomon 8:6, 7.

Many through the years have stood in the late evening at

THE END: THE UNIQUE VOICE OF ADVENTISTS

the foot of Glacier Point in Yosemite National Park, waiting for the cascade of fire to fall from the high granite cliff into the valley. The skin still prickles as one remembers that voice out of the dark, "Let the fire fall." Then, high up, another voice, through the darkness, "The fire falls."

For the world, for Seventh-day Adventists, it is fire-fall time. The Spirit of fire that burned self-centered men and women into unquenchable witnesses of the love and power of Jesus long years ago stands ready to finish His work. "Let the fire fall," should be our plea today. Fire cleanses, warms, invigorates. Christians the world over have known something of that warmth. But fires go out if not tended. And the finest steel needs more fire than boiling water.

Adventism's highest priority is to permit the fire of the Holy Spirit to consume all earthly dross, and warm their compassion for others, to invigorate their spiritual outreach so that honest seekers for truth will have no further doubts about the reality of the theology that Adventists have talked about for over a century.

God's people everywhere would then be convinced and join those "who keep the commandments of God and the faith of Jesus." God would then be fairly represented. Though evil is then unrestrained, the people of God are prepared for whatever horror, whatever surprise, whatever test of unanticipated magnitude may come.

Adventism's highest priority is to hasten that day when Jesus says, "It is finished." When the great multitude in heaven cry, " 'Hallelujah! Salvation and glory and power belong to our God, for his judgments are true and just.' " Revelation 19:1, 2. When the voice from the throne is heard, " 'Praise our God, all you his servants, you who fear him, small and great.' " Verse 5. When the voice of a great multitude rings and echoes to worlds without end: " 'Hallelujah! For the Lord our God the Almighty reigns. Let us rejoice and exult and give him the glory, for the marriage of the Lamb has come, and his Bride has made herself ready; it was granted her to be clothed with fine linen, bright and pure'—for the fine linen is the righteous deeds of the saints." Verses 6-8.

ADVENTISM'S HIGHEST PRIORITY

References

1. Ellen G. White, *Counsels to Teachers,* pp. 321, 322.
2. White, *Review and Herald,* November 23, 1905.
3. White, *Testimonies to Ministers,* p. 458. "Transformation of character is to be the testimony to the world of the indwelling love of Christ. The Lord expects His people to show that the redeeming power of grace can work upon the faulty character and cause it to develop in symmetry and abundant fruitfulness. But in order for us to fulfill God's purpose, there is a preparatory work to be done."—White, *Testimonies,* vol. 6, p. 43.
4. Ellen G. White, *Testimonies to Ministers,* pp. 511, 426.
5. White, *Testimonies,* vol. 6, p. 129.
6. White, *Testimonies,* vol. 8, pp. 153, 16.
7. White, *Testimonies,* vol. 8, p. 200.
8. White, *Testimonies,* vol. 7, pp. 142, 144.
9. Ellen G. White Comments, *S.D.A. Bible Commentary,* vol. 1, pp. 1104, 1105.
10. Ellen G. White, *Review and Herald,* October 9, 1894.
11. White, *Counsels to Teachers.*(Mountain View, Calif.: Pacific Press Publishing Association, 1913), p. 532. "We are to be as signs in the world, testifying to the power of divine grace to refine and ennoble those who give themselves to God's service." Ellen G. White Comments, *S.D.A. Bible Commentary,* vol. 2, p. 1026. "We are to accept Christ as our efficiency, our strength, that we may reveal His character to the world. This is the work resting upon us as Christians. We are to witness to the power of heavenly grace. . . . God wants His sons and daughters to reveal before the synagogue of Satan, before the heavenly universe, before the world, the power of His grace, that men and angels may know that Christ has not died in vain. Let us show the world that we have power from on high."—White, *In Heavenly Places,* p. 321.
12. White, *Testimonies,* vol. 6; pp. 9, 11-13.
13. For a sampling of such references, see: Matthew 5:16, 19, 48; 7:21; Romans 6:7, 12, 14, 17-19; 8:4; 12:2; 16:25, 26; 1 Corinthians 15:34; 2 Corinthians 12:9; Ephesians 1:12; 3:10, 16-19; 4:13, 15, 23, 24; 6:10, 11, 16; Colossians 1:10, 11, 22, 28; 1 Thessalonians 3:13; 1 Timothy 6:14; Titus 2:14; 1 Peter 1:15; 2:24; 2 Peter 1:9; 3:11-14; 1 John 3:3, 7; Jude 24; Revelation 2:7, 11, 17, 26; 3:5, 12, 21; 14:12.
14. Revelation 14:12. See chapter seven of this book for a fuller review.
15. Ellen G. White, *In Heavenly Places* (Washington D.C.: Review and Herald Publishing Association, 1967), p. 326.
16. White, *The Great Controversy,* p. 488.
17. *Ibid.,* pp. 424, 425.
18. *Ibid.,* p. 425. Emphasis supplied.
19. *Ibid.,* pp. 488, 489.
20. White, *Testimonies,* vol. 1, pp. 186, 187. "Because the time is ap-

THE END: THE UNIQUE VOICE OF ADVENTISTS

parently extended, many have become careless and indifferent in regard to their words and actions. They do not realize their danger, and do not see and understand that they may have time to form characters for the future, immortal life. Every moment is of the highest value. Time is granted them, not to be employed in studying their own ease and becoming dwellers on the earth, but to be used in the work of overcoming every defect in their own characters, and in helping others, by example and personal effort, to see the beauty of holiness."—White, *Testimonies*, vol. 4, pp. 306, 307.

21. Vernon C. Grounds, "Getting Into Shape Spiritually," *Christianity Today*, February 2, 1979.

22. White, *Christ's Object Lessons*, p. 331.

23. *Ibid.*, p. 315.

24. "Character cannot be changed when Christ comes, nor just as a man is about to die. Character building must be done in this life. We fear that repentance will come to the self-indulgent, tainted soul all too late. A few resolves, a few tears, will never reverse a guilty past life nor blot out of the books of heaven the transgressions, the willful, knowing sins of those who have had the precious light of truth, and can explain the Scriptures to others, while sin and iniquity are drunk up like stolen waters. As though written with an iron pen, they may be found *lead* in the rock forever."—White, *Testimonies to Ministers*, p. 430.

25. Ellen G. White, *Testimonies*, vol. 2, pp. 355, 356. See also White, *Testimonies*, vol. 1, pp. 185-195; vol. 4, p. 429; vol. 5, p. 466.

Appendix A

ELLEN G. WHITE STATEMENTS REGARDING A DELAYED ADVENT

Ellen G. White statements regarding the end of time, especially in reference to a waiting period, a delayed advent, are here given in chronological order. Although the following quotations present a relatively complete outline of her thought over many decades, the list is not exhaustive:

1. (1850) I saw that the time for Jesus to be in the most holy place was nearly finished and that time can last but a very little longer. . . . Live and act wholly in reference to the coming of the Son of man. The sealing time is short, and will soon be over. Now is the time, while the four angels are holding the four winds, to make our calling and election sure.—*Early Writings,* p. 58.

2. (1851) I saw that many were neglecting the preparation so needful and were looking to the time of "refreshing" and the "latter rain" to fit them to stand in the day of the Lord and to live in His sight. Oh, how many I saw in the time of trouble without a shelter! They had neglected the needful preparation; therefore they could not receive the refreshing that all must have to fit them to live in the sight of a Holy God.—*Early Writings,* p. 71.

3. (1859) I was shown that the testimony to the Laodiceans applies to God's people at the present time, and the reason it has not accomplished a greater work is because of the hardness of their hearts. But God has given the message time to do its work. The heart must be purified from sins which have so long shut out Jesus. . . . Nearly all believed that this message would end in the loud cry of the third angel. But as they failed to see the powerful work accomplished in a short time, many lost the effect of the message. I saw that this message would not accomplish its work in a few short months. . . . If the message had been of as short duration as many of us supposed, there would have been no time for them to develop character.—*Testimonies,* vol. 1, pp. 186, 187.

THE END: THE UNIQUE VOICE OF ADVENTISTS

4. (1865) I was shown that our Sabbathkeeping people have been negligent in acting upon the light which God has given in regard to the health reform, that there is yet a great work before us. . . . I was shown that the work of health reform has scarcely been entered upon yet. . . . The health reform, I was shown, is a part of the third angel's message and is just as closely connected with it as are the arm and hand with the human body. I saw that we as a people must make an advance move in this great work. . . . God's people are not prepared for the loud cry of the third angel.—*Testimonies,* vol. 1, pp. 485, 486.

5. (1868) The long night of gloom is trying; but the morning is deferred in mercy, because if the Master should come, so many would be found unready. God's unwillingness to have His people perish has been the reason for so long delay.—*Testimonies,* vol. 2, p. 194.

6. (1883) It is true that time has continued longer than we expected in the early days of this message. Our Saviour did not appear as soon as we hoped. But has the word of the Lord failed? Never! It should be remembered that the promises and threatenings of God are alike conditional.

God had committed to His people a work to be accomplished on earth. The third angel's message was to be given, the minds of believers were to be directed to the heavenly sanctuary, where Christ had entered to make atonement for His people. The Sabbath reform was to be carried forward. . . . The message must be proclaimed with a loud voice, that all the inhabitants of earth might receive the warning. The people of God must purify their souls through obedience to the truth, and be prepared to stand without fault before Him at His coming.

Had Adventists, after the great disappointment in 1844, held fast their faith, and followed on unitedly in the opening providence of God, receiving the message of the third angel and in the power of the Holy Spirit proclaiming it to the world, they would have seen the salvation of God, the Lord would have wrought mightily with their efforts, the work would have been completed, and Christ would have come ere this to receive His people to their reward.

But in the period of doubt and uncertainty that followed the disappointment, many of the advent believers yielded their faith. . . . Had the whole Adventist body united upon the commandments

APPENDIX A

of God and the faith of Jesus, how widely different would have been our history!

It was not the will of God that the coming of Christ should be thus delayed. God did not design that His people, Israel, should wander forty years in the wilderness. . . .

The same sins have delayed the entrance of modern Israel into the heavenly Canaan. In neither case were the promises of God at fault. It is the unbelief, the worldliness, unconsecration, and strife among the Lord's professed people that have kept us in this world of sin and sorrow so many years.—*Selected Messages*, bk. 1, pp. 67-69.

7. (1884) If all who had labored unitedly in the work in 1844, had received the third angel's message and proclaimed it in the power of the Holy Spirit, the Lord would have wrought mightily with their efforts. A flood of light would have been shed upon the world. Years ago the inhabitants of the earth would have been warned, the closing work completed, and Christ would have come for the redemption of His people.

It was not the will of God that Israel should wander forty years in the wilderness; He desired to lead them directly to the land of Canaan and establish them there, a holy, happy people. But "they could not enter in because of unbelief." Hebrews 3:19. Because of their backsliding and apostasy they perished in the desert, and others were raised up to enter the Promised Land. In like manner, it was not the will of God that the coming of Christ should be so long delayed and His people should remain so many years in this world of sin and sorrow. But unbelief separated them from God. As they refused to do the work which He had appointed them, others were raised up to proclaim the message. In mercy to the world, Jesus delays His coming, that sinners may have an opportunity to hear the warning and find in Him a shelter before the wrath of God shall be poured out.—*Spirit of Prophecy*, vol. 4, pp. 291, 292; *The Great Controversy*, p. 458.

8. (1888) A great crisis awaits the people of God. A crisis awaits the world. The most momentous struggle of all the ages is just before us. Events which for more than forty years we have upon the authority of the prophetic word declared to be impending are now taking place before our eyes.—*Testimonies*, vol. 5, p. 711. (Reference to National Sunday Law legislation.)

THE END: THE UNIQUE VOICE OF ADVENTISTS

9. (1892) You will not be able to say that He will come in one, two, or five years, neither are you to put off His coming by stating that it may not be for ten or twenty years.—*Review and Herald,* March 22, 1892.

10. (1892) The work is soon to close. The members of the church militant who have proved faithful will become the church triumphant.—*Evangelism,* p. 707.

11. (1895) The descent of the Holy Spirit upon the church is looked forward to as in the future; but it is the privilege of the church to have it now. Seek for it, pray for it, believe for it. We must have it, and Heaven is waiting to bestow it.—*Review and Herald,* March 19, 1895.

12. (1896) Every truly converted soul will be intensely desirous to bring others from the darkness of error into the marvelous light of the righteousness of Jesus Christ. The great outpouring of the Spirit of God, which lightens the whole earth with His glory, will not come until we have an enlightened people, that know by experience what it means to be laborers together with God. When we have entire, whole-hearted consecration to the service of Christ, God will recognize the fact by an outpouring of his Spirit without measure; but this will not be while the largest portion of the church are not laborers together with God.—*Review and Herald,* July 21, 1896.

13. (1896) If those who claimed to have a living experience in the things of God had done their appointed work as the Lord ordained, the whole world would have been warned ere this and the Lord Jesus would have come in power and great glory.—*Review and Herald,* Oct. 6, 1896.

14. (1897) Ever since the proclamation of the third angel's message, angels of God have been waiting to cooperate with the human agent who is in earnest and determined to work.—*Testimony to Ministers,* p. 123.

15. (1898) By giving the gospel to the world it is in our power to hasten our Lord's return. We are not only to look for but to hasten the coming of the day of God. 2 Peter 3:12, margin. Had the church of Christ done her appointed work as the Lord ordained, the whole world would before this have been warned, and the Lord Jesus would have come to our earth in power and great glory.—*The Desire of Ages,* pp. 633, 634.

APPENDIX A

16. (1898) Had the purpose of God been carried out by His people in giving the message of mercy to the world, Christ would have come to the earth, and the saints would ere this have received their welcome into the city of God.—*Australian Union Record,* October 15, 1898.

17. (1900) When all are faithful in giving back to God His own in tithes and offerings, the way will be opened for the world to hear the message for this time. If the hearts of God's people were filled with love for Christ; if every church member were thoroughly imbued with the Spirit of self-sacrifice; if all manifested thorough earnestness, there would be no lack of funds for home or foreign missions. Our resources would be multiplied; a thousand doors of usefulness would be opened, and we should be invited to enter. Had the purpose of God been carried out by His people in giving to the world the message of mercy, Christ would, ere this, have come to the earth, and the saints would have received their welcome into the city of God.—*Testimonies,* vol. 6, p. 450.

18. (1900) Christ is waiting with longing desire for the manifestation of Himself in His church. When the character of Christ shall be perfectly reproduced in His people, then He will come to claim them as His own. It is the privilege of every Christian not only to look for, but to hasten the coming of our Lord Jesus Christ. Were all who profess His name bearing fruit to His glory, how quickly the whole world would be sown with the seed of the gospel. Quickly the last great harvest would be ripened, and Christ would come to gather the precious grain.—*Christ's Object Lessons,* p. 69.

19. (1900) We are standing upon the threshold of great and solemn events. Prophecies are fulfilling. Strange, eventful history is being recorded in the books of heaven. Everything in our world is in agitation. . . . The nations are angry, and the time of the dead has come, that they should be judged. Events are changing to bring about the day of God, which hasteth greatly. Only a moment of time, as it were, yet remains.—*Testimonies,* vol. 6, p. 14.

20. (1901) It [the coming of the Lord] will not tarry past the time that the message is borne to all nations, tongues, and peoples. Shall we who claim to be students of prophecy forget that God's forbearance to the wicked is a part of the vast and merciful plan by which He is seeking to compass the salvation of souls?—*Review and Herald,* June 18, 1901.

21. (1901) We may have to remain here in this world because of insubordination many more years, as did the children of Israel; but for Christ's sake, His people should not add sin to sin by charging God with the consequence of their own wrong course of action.—Letter 184, 1901; *Evangelism*, p. 696.

22. (1902) We are nearing the end of this earth's history, and the different lines of God's work are to be carried forward with much more self-sacrifice than is at present manifest.... In all parts of the world a work that should have been done long ago is now to be entered upon and carried forward to completion.—*Testimonies*, vol. 7, p. 52.

23. (1902) The goodly fabric of character wrought through divine power will receive light and glory from heaven, and will stand out before the world as a witness, pointing to the throne of the living God. Then the work will move forward with solidity and double strength. A new efficiency will be imparted to the workers in every line. Men will learn of the reconciliation from iniquity which the Messiah has brought in through His sacrifice. The last message of warning and salvation will be given with mighty power. The earth will be lightened with the glory of God, and it will be ours to witness the soon coming, in power and glory, of our Lord and Saviour.—*Medical Ministry*, p. 185.

24. (1903) I know that if the people of God had preserved a living connection with Him, if they had obeyed His Word, they could today be in the heavenly Canaan.—*General Conference Bulletin*, March 30, 1903; *Evangelism*, p. 694.

25. (1903) The day is at hand. For the lesson to be learned, the work to be done, the transformation of character to be effected, the time remaining is but too brief a span.—*Education*, p. 184.

26. (1903) In order to destroy sin and its results He gave His best Beloved, and He has put it in our power, through co-operation with Him, to bring this scene of misery to an end. "This gospel of the kingdom shall be preached in all the world for a witness unto all nations; and then shall the end come." Matthew 24:14.—*Education*, p. 264.

27. (1904) If all who had labored unitedly in the work of 1844 had received the third angel's message and proclaimed it in the power of the Holy Spirit, the Lord would have wrought mightily with their efforts. A flood of light would have been shed upon the world.

APPENDIX A

Years ago the inhabitants of the earth would have been warned, the closing work would have been completed, and Christ would have come [before 1904] for the redemption of His people—*Testimonies,* vol. 8, p. 116.

28. (1905) Angels are now restraining the winds of strife, until the world shall be warned of its coming doom; but a storm is gathering, ready to burst upon the earth, and when God shall bid his angels loose the winds, there will be such a scene of strife as no pen can picture. . . . A moment of respite has been graciously given us of God. Every power lent us of heaven is to be used in doing the work assigned us by the Lord for those who are perishing in ignorance.—*Review and Herald,* November 23, 1905.

29. (1909) If every watchman on the walls of Zion had given the trumpet a certain sound, the world might ere this have heard the message of warning. But the work is years behind. While men have slept, Satan has stolen a march upon us.—*Testimonies,* vol. 9, p. 29.

30. (1909) There will be a series of events revealing that God is master of the situation. The truth will be proclaimed in clear, unmistakable language. As a people we must prepare the way of the Lord under the overruling guidance of the Holy Spirit. The gospel is to be given in its purity. The stream of living water is to deepen and widen in its course. In all fields, nigh and afar off, men will be called from the plow and from the more common commercial business vocations that largely occupy the mind, and will be educated in connection with men of experience. As they learn to labor effectively they will proclaim the truth with power. Through most wonderful workings of divine providence, mountains of difficulty will be removed and cast into the sea. The message that means so much to the dwellers upon the earth will be heard and understood. Men will know what is truth. Onward and still onward the work will advance until the whole earth shall have been warned, and then shall the end come.—*Testimonies,* vol. 9, p. 96.

31. (1911) When the members of the church of God do their appointed work in the needy fields at home and abroad, in fulfillment of the gospel commission, the whole world will soon be warned and the Lord Jesus will return to this earth with power and great glory.—*The Acts of the Apostles,* p. 111.

Appendix B

STATEMENTS OF IMMINENT ADVENT THROUGH THE CENTURIES

One of the most sobering facts throughout the history of the Christian church is that men and women have periodically interpreted the conditions of the world in their day to be fulfillments of prophecy and clear signs of the end. Some of these statements are here listed, not to direct ridicule at the writers, but to join them in commitment and seriousness—all the while learning an important lesson:

A. Period from A.D. 100 to 1300

1. *Clement of Rome* (ca 100) "Of a truth, soon and suddenly shall His will be accomplished, as the Scriptures also bear witness, saying, 'Speedily will He come, and will not tarry;' and, 'The Lord shall suddenly come to His temple, even the Holy One, for whom ye look.' "—"First Epistle to Corinthians," chapter 23, in *Ante-Nicene Fathers (ANF)*, vol. 1, p. 11.

"Let us therefore earnestly strive to be found in the number of those that wait for Him." *Ibid.*, chap. 35, p. 14.

2. *Ignatius* (ca 108) "These are the last times; let us feel shame, let us fear the patience of God, that it may not result in our condemnation."—"Epistle to the Ephesians," chapter 11, Goodspeed, *The Apostolic Fathers*, p. 210.

"Understand the times. Wait for him who is above time, timeless, invisible, yet visible for our sakes."—"Epistle to Polycarp," chap. 3, p. 233.

3. *Barnabas* (ca 130) "The day is near when all things will perish with the Evil One. The Lord is at hand, with his reward."—"Epistle of Barnabas," chap. 21, p. 45

4. *Cyprian* (200?-258) "Whatever things were predicted are fulfilled;... the end of the world is approaching."—*Treatise* I, par. 16, *ANF*, vol. 5, p. 426.

"The world has now grown old.... The whole world itself

APPENDIX B

is already in process of failing, and in its end. . . . The day of judgment is now drawing nigh."—*Treatise* V, par. 3, 4, 5, ANF, vol. 5, p. 459.

"That wars continue frequently to prevail, that death and famine accumulate anxiety, that health is shattered by raging diseases, that the human race is wasted by the desolation of pestilence, know that this was foretold; that evils should be multiplied in the last times, and that misfortunes should be varied; and that as the day of judgment is now drawing nigh, the censure of an indignant God should be more and more aroused for the scourging of the human race."—*Treatise* V, par. 5, in *ANF*, vol. 5, p. 459.

"The kingdom of God, beloved brethren, is beginning to be at hand; the reward of life, and the rejoicing of eternal salvation, and the perpetual gladness and possession lately lost of paradise, are now coming, with the passing away of the world. . . . It is for him to fear death who is not willing to go to Christ. It is for him to be unwilling to go to Christ who does not believe that he is about to reign with Christ."—*Treatise* VII, par. 2, *ANF*, vol. 5, p. 469.

5. *Ambrose* (340?-397) "The gospel is preached that the world may be destroyed; for the preaching of the gospel has gone out into the whole world, and therefore we see the end of the world approaching." Cited in Daniel Taylor, *The Reign of Christ on Earth* (Boston: H. L. Hastings, 1881), p. 92.

6. *Sulpicius Severus* (ca 363-425) "Finally, by the clay and the iron being mixed together, yet never in their substance thoroughly uniting, are shadowed forth those futures of the human race which disagree among themselves, though apparently combined. . . . And the prophets declare that these are the last times." *Post-Nicene Fathers (PNF)* 2nd series, vol. 11, p. 98.

7. *Gregory the Great* (ca 540-604) "We learn from the words of the Almighty Lord in Holy Scripture, the end of the present world is already close at hand, and the reign of the saints is coming, which can have no end. And now that this end of the world is approaching, many things are at hand which previously have not been; to wit, changes of the air, terrors from heaven, and seasons contrary to the accustomed order of times, wars, famine, pestilences, earthquakes in divers places. Yet these things will not come in our days, but after our days they will all ensue. You therefore, if you observe any of these things occurring in your land,

by no means let your mind be troubled, since these signs of the end of the world are sent beforehand for this purpose, that we should be solicitous about our souls, suspectful of the hour of death and in our good deeds be found prepared for the coming Judge." *PNF,* bk. 11, ep. 66, vol. 13, p. 82.

"Indeed among the clergy and people of this city there has been such an invasion of feverous sicknesses that hardly any freeman, hardly any slave, remains fit for any office ministry. Moreover, from the neighbouring cities we have news daily of havocs and of mortality. Then, how Africa is being wasted by mortality and sickness I believe that you know more accurately than we do, insomuch as you are nearer to it. But of the East those who come from thence report still more grievous desolations. In the midst of all these things, therefore, since you perceive that there is a general smiting as the end of the world draws near, you ought not to be too much afflicted for your own troubles." Gregory, *PNF,* bk. 9, ep. 123, vol. 13, p. 27.

    8. *Emphasis on the year 1000 A.D.* Working on the concept that the 6000th year of time would end about the year 1000 A.D., the Roman church persuaded owners of large areas of land in Europe to donate their possessions to the church in exchange for the assurance of pardon for their sins. The transfer deeds contained this clause: "Appropinquante mundi termino," that is, "as the end of the world is approaching." Jesse Forrest Silver, *The Lord's Return* (New York: Fleming H. Revell, 1914), p. 110.

    "O Brethren, give ear to a noble Lesson.
We ought always to watch and pray,
For we see the World nigh to a conclusion.
We ought to strive to do good works,
Seeing that the end of this World approacheth.
There are already *a thousand and one hundred
    years fully accomplished,*
Since it was written thus, *For we are in the
    last time."* Samuel Morland, *The History of the Evangelical Churches of the Valleys of Piedmont,* p. 99 cited in Froom, *Prophetic Faith of Our Fathers* (Washington D.C.: Review and Herald Publishing Association, 1946), vol. I, p. 872.

  B. Period from 1300 to 1800

    1. *John Wycliffe* (1320?-1384) "The Last Age of the

APPENDIX B

Church" is the title of a tract which was never printed; its manuscript may be found in the Library of Trinity College, Dublin. Wycliffe wrote this tract during a period of widespread earthquakes and ravaging pestilences, which, according to some records, killed off one third of the population of Europe. He thus believed that these terrible events were indeed signs of the end of the world and that the fourteenth century would usher in the advent. See Froom, *Prophetic Faith,* vol. II, pp. 58, 59.

2. *Columbus* (1451-1506) "The greatest part of the prophecies and (of) the Holy Scriptures is already finished. . . .

"I said above that much remained for the completion of the prophecies, and I say that there are great things in the world, and I say that the sign is that Our Lord is hastening them; the preaching of this gospel in so many lands, in recent times, tells it to me." Froom, *Prophetic Faith of our Fathers,* vol. II, pp. 174, 175.

3. *Martin Luther* (1483-1546) "Printing is the latest and greatest gift, by which God enables us to advance the things of the Gospel. It is the last bright flame, manifesting itself just previous to the extinction of the world. Thanks be to God, it came before the last day came." Jules Michelet, *Life of Luther* (London: David Bogue, 1846), p. 291.

"I know more than thou [Melancthon] dost about the destiny of our world; that destiny is destruction; it is inevitably so—seeing how triumphantly the devil walks about, and how mankind grow daily worse and worse. There is one consolation, that the day of judgment is quite close at hand. The Word of God has become a wearisome thing to man, a thing viewed with disgust. . . . Nothing remains but to pray: 'thy will be done.' " *Ibid.,* p. 344.

"All around me I observe an unconquerable cupidity prevalent; this is another of the signs which convince me that the last day is at hand; it seems as though the world in its old age, its last paroxysm, was growing delirious, as sometimes happens to dying people." *Ibid.*

4. *Melanchthon* (1497-1560) In the British Museum is a copy of the first edition of Luther's German Bible, in two volumes. The following words are written upon the third page of the flyleaf of the second volume, in the handwriting of Melanchthon:

"Written in the year 1557, after the birth of our Lord Jesus Christ of the Virgin Mary. Year from the creation of the world, 5519. From this number we may be assured that this aged world is not far from its end." Taylor, *The Reign of Christ on Earth*, p. 160.

5. *Hugh Latimer* (1490-1555) " 'The Lord will not come till the swerving from faith cometh:' which thing is already done and past. Antichrist is known throughout all the world. Wherefore the day is not far off. Let us beware, for it will one day fall upon our heads." *Works*, vol. 1, p. 356, in Froom, *Prophetic Faith of our Fathers*, vol. II, p. 371.

"Therefore all those excellent learned men, which without doubt God hath sent into this world in these latter days to give the world warning, all those men do gather out of the scripture that the last day cannot be far off." *Works*, vol. 2, p. 365, in Froom, *Prophetic Faith of our Fathers*, vol. II, p. 372.

6. *Nicholas Ridley* (1500?-1555) "The world without doubt—this I do believe and therefore I say it—draws towards an end. Let us, with John, the servant of God, cry in our hearts unto our Saviour Christ, Come, Lord Jesus, come." "Lamentation for the Change of Religion," cited in Taylor, *The Reign of Christ on Earth*, p. 145.

7. *John Foxe* (1517-1587), the author of *The Book of Martyrs*, is quoted by Elliott as believing that the advent of Christ "could not be very far off from the time then present." E. B. Elliott, *Horae Apocalypticas*, vol. II, p. 142.

8. *Samuel Rutherford* (1600-1661) "The day is near the dawning.... Christ will be on us in haste.... Watch but a little and, ere long, the skies shall rend . . . and Jesus will come in the clouds. . . . The day of the Lord is near at hand." Cited in Silver, *The Lord's Return*, p. 175.

9. *Richard Baxter* (1651-1691) "We daily behold the forerunners of his coming foretold by himself. We see the fig tree putteth forth leaves, and therefore know that summer is nigh. Though the riotous would say my Lord delayeth his coming, yet the saints lift up their heads, for their redemption draweth nigh. Alas! fellow Christians, what should we do if our Lord should not return?"—*The Saint's Everlasting Rest* (New York, N.Y.: American Tract Society, n.d.), p. 42.

10. *John Wesley* (1703-1791) "We are very shortly to expect, one after another, the calamities occasioned by the second

APPENDIX B

beast, the harvest and the vintage; the pouring out of the vials, the judgment of Babylon, the last raging of the beast and his destruction, the imprisonment of Satan. How great things those! And how short the time! . . .

"This fulfillment (Satan's building) approaches nearer and nearer, and contains things of the utmost importance, the knowledge of which becomes every day more distinct and easy."—*Notes on the New Testament* (New York, N.Y.: Carlton and Phillips, 1854), p. 438.

    11. *William Cowper* (1731-1809)
"In a world that seems
To toll the death-bell of its own decease.
And by the voice of all its elements
To preach the general doom. When were winds
Let slip with such a warrant to destroy?
When did the waves so haughtily o'erleap
Their ancient barrier, deluging the dry?
Fires from beneath, and meteors from above,
Portentous, unexampled, unexplained,
Have kindled beacons in the skies, and the old
And crazy earth has had her shaking fits
More frequent, and foregone her usual rest.
Is it time to wrangle, when the props
And pillars of our planet seem to fail,
And nature (seems) with dim and sickly eye
To wait the close of all?" *The Poetical Works of William Cowper,* "Task" (London: William P. Nimno, 1875), bk. 2, p. 52.

    12. *The Gentlemen's Magazine,* 1756 "This most tremendous judgment and dreadful catastrophe [Lisbon earthquake] that has now suddenly overtaken these deluded peoples, when reposed in a fatal and hopeless security, at so very critical a juncture and moment of time, attended with so many other very observable circumstances, cannot as I think, fail to awaken all the world to serious and devout contemplations . . . and I doubt not, hath set many to compare it with the prophecies relating to, and now fulfilling in these its last days.

    "This species of calamity, so multiplied and magnified as it is, and of the most striking and terrifying kind, we ought surely to look upon as one of the infallible omens and forebodings of the

THE END: THE UNIQUE VOICE OF ADVENTISTS

pangs of nature in her sickening state." January 1756, p. 68.
  C. Period from 1800 to present
    1. *Horatius Bonar* (1808-1889)
    "Time's sun is fast setting, its twilight is nigh.
    Its evening is falling in cloud o'er the sky:
    Its shadows are stretching in ominous gloom,
    Its midnight approaches, the midnight of doom.
    Then haste, sinner, haste, there is mercy for thee;
    And wrath is preparing, flee, lingerer, flee." Cited in Taylor, *The Reign of Christ,* p. xxxii.
    2. The testimonies of the leaders in the Great Advent Awakening of the early 1800s, such as William Miller, Josiah Litch, Joshua Himes, et al, are well known.
    3. *Editorial in Harper's Weekly.* "It is a gloomy moment in history. Not for many years—not in the lifetime of most men who read this paper—has there been so much grave and deep apprehension; never has the future seemed so incalculable as at this time. In our own country there is a universal commercial prostration and panic and thousands of our poorest fellow-citizens are burned out against the approaching winter without employment, and without the prospects of it. In France the political caldron seethes and bubbles with uncertainty; Russia hangs as usual, like a cloud dark and silent upon the horizon of Europe; while all the energies, resources and influences of the British Empire are sorely tried, and are yet to be tried more sorely. . . .

    "It is a solemn moment, and no man can feel an indifference—which, happily, no man pretends to feel,—in the issue of events. Of our own troubles no man can see the end. They are fortunately, as yet mainly commercial, and if we are only to lose money, and by painful poverty to be taught wisdom—the wisdom of honor, of faith, of sympathy, and of charity—no man need seriously to despair. And yet the very haste to be rich, which is the occasion of this wide-spread calamity, has also tended to destroy the moral forces with which we are to resist and subdue the calamity." October 10, 1857.

    "The sun is setting—the air is chill—health is failing; there are no stars—there is only universal ignorance, regret, grief, and despair. It is easy enough to say that we are in the woods; it is easy to see that we are—for a time at least—lost; it is not difficult to

APPENDIX B

know that we came in of our own accord." October 17, 1857.

4. Innumerable references exist since the late nineteenth century, increasing in intensity and number, as years pass, that call every war since the Russo-Japanese Conflict the sign of the end. Daniel's one world, plus other prophecies of world confederation in the very end of time, have been identified as League of Nations, United Nations, The Common Market, NATO, and similar entities. The antichrist has been variously identified as some historical personality, including Henry Kissinger, Hitler, Stalin, and Mussolini. The termination of the "times of the Gentiles" has been given several dates. The recital is long. One of the most complete books currently dealing with these subjects is Dwight Wilson's, *Armageddon Now!* (Grand Rapids, Mich.: Baker Book House, 1977).

Appendix C

A PLAUSIBLE SCENARIO

A small publication called *Table Talk* is frequently placed before each customer in a well-known Washington, D.C., restaurant. One of the issues (December 1977) contained a short article, "A Glimpse Into the Future." It caught our breath, for it may well be the scenario that all the world will participate in not many years from now:

"It is mid-December in the year 1990. We are seated with our reporters in the main assembly room of what was once the United Nations Building. The name has been changed to the United World Building, for now, every nation on earth has representation here.

"This is a momentous occasion, for a whole new section has been added to accommodate religious leaders of the world. It had long been felt that the original UN was purely political in structure, whereas many of man's problems stemmed from religious differences.

"Members and spectators seem excited. Never before, in the history of man, have so many representatives of so many religions gathered together in one spot. There is a constant droning sound as the many members exchange remarks with one another. Suddenly, the great hall is hushed. A tall, beautifully-groomed woman walks slowly and gracefully towards the podium. She is wearing a pleated, white dress, and long white gloves. She is Madame Colombe La Paix, Chairman of the United World assembly and a Nobel Peace Prize winner in 1989."

The columnist proceeded to imagine the possible message that this world peace leader would deliver on this great occasion. " 'For centuries—too many centuries—man had waged war with his neighbors for reasons of conquest, for expansion, or for political and religious differences. And now, with the incorporation of the Coalition of World Religions, we feel we will be able to over-

APPENDIX C

come the final barrier to a lasting world peace.

" 'Every active religion on earth is represented here today and the basis of each of these religions is belief in a Surpreme Being. Each, then, and the majority of us in this assemblage, have a common bond and firm foundation upon which we can hope to reconcile present and future national and international religious differences. . . .

" 'I ask, humbly and sincerely, that each religious leader here today pledge to work with the others for a true religious peace and understanding, for by whatever name each of us uses when speaking of the God of us all, He is just that—*The God of Us All.*

" 'When this entire assembly attains a true cooperative world peace so that men will no longer be afraid of one another, then they can concentrate their unlimited energies and resources toward making this a better world for *all* in it.' "

Such is the columnist's view of how the world will solve its problems. In 1979 it is not farfetched, although it probably could not have been written before the dizzying events of the past twenty years.

Appendix D

ANNUAL COUNCIL APPEALS, 1973 AND 1974

1973

We believe that the return of Jesus has been long delayed, that the reasons for the delay are not wrapped in mysteries, and that the primary consideration before the Seventh-day Adventist Church is to reorder its priorities individually and corporately so that our Lord's return may be hastened.

We are not the first leaders in Adventist history to feel the urgency of preparing the church for the fullness of the "latter rain" experience, the "loud cry of the third angel's message," and the triumphal return of the awaited Lord. Often God's special messenger to the remnant people made this appeal. Especially specific were her words written in 1892:

"The loud cry of the third angel has already begun in the revelation of the righteousness of Christ, the sin-pardoning Redeemer. This is the beginning of the light of the angel whose glory shall fill the whole earth."—*Christ Our Righteousness,* p. 56. This statement is an inspired declaration that the fulfilling of Revelation 18:1-4, in which "another angel" joins the three angels of Revelation 14:6-12 in lightening the whole earth with their glory, had begun. In the four years following the historic Minneapolis General Conference, the fresh, compelling emphasis on "righteousness by faith" had aroused the Adventist Church in such a way that Ellen White could say that the "loud cry" had begun!

One question therefore, has overshadowed all other subjects at this 1973 Annual Council: What has happened to the message and experience that by 1892 had brought the beginning of earth's final message of warning and appeal?

Although in our earnest search for answers we have no disposition to blame those to whom the message first came, nor those who have led in the work from then until now, we have been determined to discover any pitfalls in our past history that may be avoided

APPENDIX D

today and to profit by such lessons.

But more than all else we are persuaded that it is the *present* experience that is of primary concern—the way from past inadequacy to rapid triumph. It has been "latter rain" time for many years!

We are not unaware of the fact that all through our ranks many of our members enjoy a rich, victorious experience. They have received the early rain experience and are rejoicing in the Lord. But this is no cause for complacency or exaltation. As a body the church still is in the Laodicean condition as set forth by the True Witness in Revelation 3:14-19. Therefore, in attempting to find the specific present causes for failure and delay, the council has noted three main factors:

1. Leaders and people have not fully accepted as a personal message Christ's analysis and appeal to the Laodiceans (Rev. 3:14-22).

2. Leaders and people are in some ways disobedient to divine directives, both in personal experience and in the conduct of the church's commission.

3. Leaders and people have not yet finished the church's task.

Because the latter rain experience has not yet come, delegates at this Annual Council have been driven to the conclusion that the message of Christ to the Laodiceans has not been clearly understood or adequately heeded. The climax of the sequence of events predicted in the following quotation has not been reached, indicating that there is yet need for a people to fulfill the requirements of the True Witness: "Those who come up to every point, and stand every test, and overcome, be the price what it may, have heeded the counsel of the True Witness, and they will receive the latter rain, and thus be fitted for translation."—*Testimonies,* vol. 1, p. 187.

The message to Laodicea involves a personal relationship to Jesus Christ that will produce a quality people, a conquering people, a people who, in Christ's own words, will conquer "as I myself conquered" (Rev. 3:21, R.S.V.). This message will produce a people whom God can set forth without embarrassment as exhibits of those who "keep the commandments of God and the faith of Jesus" (Rev. 14:12, R.S.V.), a people who have learned through experience that all goodness is a result of being sustained

THE END: THE UNIQUE VOICE OF ADVENTISTS

by divine power. Such people can be entrusted with special power because they will use it the way Jesus used power; indeed, in all aspects of life they will reflect the character of Jesus.

Becoming like Jesus in word and deed is the goal of the process called "righteousness by faith": "The righteousness of Christ is not a cloak to cover unconfessed and unforsaken sin; it is a principle of life that transforms the character and controls the conduct. Holiness is wholeness for God; it is the entire surrender of heart and life to the indwelling of the principles of heaven."—*The Desire of Ages,* pp. 555, 556.

As delegates to this Annual Council we believe that this is the heart of the church's need—understanding and experiencing all that is meant by the phrase, "righteousness by faith." Such righteousness is God's will lived out by continual faith in His power. God is waiting for a generation of Adventists who will demonstrate that His way of life can truly be lived on earth, that Jesus did not set an example beyond the reach of His followers, that His grace "is able to keep you from falling and to present you without blemish" (Jude 24, R.S.V.).

Each member of the Laodicean church needs more than a theoretical knowledge or even a proof-text knowledge of the Word; he needs a genuine and complete surrender of the life and will to the divine authority of the Bible and of the Spirit of Prophecy—a surrender that may well call for revolutionary changes in personal life-styles and in denominational policies and practices. Every member must recognize that he has a part in either hastening or delaying the coming of Christ. Says God's servant: "When the character of Christ shall be perfectly reproduced in His people, then He will come to claim them as His own."—*Christ's Object Lessons,* p. 69.

As church leaders at this Annual Council we have faced honestly the fact that there are inconsistencies between the church's preaching and its practices, and to allow these inconsistencies to continue will automatically delay the completion of the church's mission and the coming of Christ.

God has in love sent to the Seventh-day Adventist Church inspired counsels that illuminate and apply the words of Scripture. These counsels cover about every conceivable facet of Christian experience and witness. As Seventh-day Adventists we cannot

APPENDIX D

plead ignorance of God's will concerning His expectations, either for the individual or for the church. If we ignore or reject God's counsels, this may well be defined as an act of insubordination, which will affect our relation to the coming of the Lord. In the words of God's servant: "We may have to remain here in this world because of insubordination many more years, as did the children of Israel."—*Evangelism,* p. 696.

At this Annual Council small study groups of church leaders have earnestly examined areas of possible failure to follow divine counsel. They have pointed up the need for greater care in Sabbath observance, in stewardship of God's gifts, in guarding the avenues of the soul, and in practicing the broad and specific principles of healthful living. On the latter question they have taken seriously the inspired statement: "This is a work that will have to be done before His [God's] people can stand before Him a perfected people."—*Testimonies,* vol. 9, p. 154.

These study groups also have pointed to evidences of sagging morality, including a more casual attitude toward divorce and remarriage. Concern has been expressed over the increasing tendency to imitate the world in dress and ornamentation.

These study groups have examined the whole spectrum of Seventh-day Adventist institutional work and have pointed to evidences that some institutions in various respects are losing their distinctive character as instrumentalities for the furtherance of God's work on earth. (See *Fundamentals of Christian Education,* p. 351.) While earnest efforts have been made to reform, it is recognized that as institutions grow larger, the difficulty of reforming is greater.

It is recognized that in an age of growing social consciousness and change, Adventist institutions may become involved in worthy endeavors in which the world also participates, while neglecting that work which only the church of the remnant can do. (See *Review and Herald,* Nov. 26, 1970.)

One of the greatest threats to our institutions of higher learning is seen in the counterfeit philosophies and theologies that may be unconsciously absorbed in worldly institutions by our future teachers and brought back as the "wine" of Babylon to Adventist schools (Rev. 14:8-10; 18:1-4).

It is recognized that a constant threat to spirituality grows out of

THE END: THE UNIQUE VOICE OF ADVENTISTS

increasing creature comforts, rising standards of living, and a desire for remuneration equal to that offered by the world. Wrote God's servant: "The cause of present truth was founded in self-denial and self-sacrifice. . . . We need to take heed lest we outgrow the simple, self-sacrificing spirit that marked our work in its early years."—*Selected Messages,* bk. 2, p. 197.

As the Annual Council has reviewed these and other aspects of the lives of God's people and the institutions of the church, it has raised the question as to whether much of this represents insubordination to the authority and will of God so clearly expressed through His Word and the writings of the Spirit of Prophecy. Without attempting to pinpoint areas of insubordination, the council pleads with God's people everywhere to respond to the appeal for revival and reformation—to make whatever changes may be necessary to enable the church to represent Christ adequately and fulfill its unique mission.

As delegates to this Annual Council we are much aware of one factor that delays the coming of Christ: the unfinished task of carrying the three angels' messages to the entire world (Revelation 14 and 18). We believe that Mrs. White made clear that Christ cannot come until the entire world has had a fair opportunity to hear God's saving message. For example, she wrote: "Had the purpose of God been carried out by His people in giving to the world the message of mercy, Christ would, ere this, have come."—*Testimonies,* vol. 6, p. 450.

God was willing to bring His work to a swift triumph following 1844, in 1888, and again in 1901 (among other times). Why then the delay? What can be done now?

In response to this question, the delegates at this 1973 Annual Council extend the following appeal to all workers and members throughout the world. The appeal is threefold and yet it is one:

1. Without further delay open the heart's door fully to the waiting, pleading Saviour (Rev. 3:20). Admit Jesus as the absolute Ruler of the life. Let Him enter the heart to transform it and to rule. Under the influence of the "early rain," live up to all the light you have. Put into practice all the counsel God has given you.

2. Forsake the spirit of insubordination that too long has influenced individual and church decisions. This will prepare the way for the renewal of the "latter rain" that has been delayed since the

APPENDIX D

earlier years of our history, for God cannot send the Spirit in His fullness while people disregard the counsels He has graciously sent through that same Spirit, the Spirit of Prophecy.

3. Make a new commitment to the church's task of reaching earth's billions with the three angels' messages. This commitment will call for personal dedication, for personal witnessing, for personal sacrifice. Moreover, it will call for deep intercession with God on the part of each member, a pleading with God for the "latter rain" of the Holy Spirit's power for effectual, convincing, loving witness in deed and word.

We believe that all heaven is ready to do great exploits on behalf of the church that bears God's last call of mercy. We believe that God has wonderful surprises in store for every church member who commits himself completely to Heaven's plan for a perfected people—a people that will reflect the image of Jesus fully.

That a genuine revival will come is clear from the following statement: "Before the final visitation of God's judgments upon the earth there will be among the people of the Lord such a revival of primitive godliness as has not been witnessed since apostolic times. The Spirit and power of God will be poured out upon His children."—*The Great Controversy*, p. 464. That Satan will endeavor to prevent this revival is also clear: "The enemy of souls desires to hinder this work; and before the time for such a movement shall come, he will endeavor to prevent it by introducing a counterfeit. In those churches which he can bring under his deceptive power he will make it appear that God's special blessing is poured out; there will be manifest what is thought to be a great religious interest."—*Ibid*. If the fast-spreading charismatic movement in the world today is the false revival forecast by God's Spirit, clearly the time must be near for God to pour out the latter rain upon his remnant people.

Therefore, we appeal to our church members everywhere to join hands with conference workers and church officers in a great revival and reformation that will enable God to reveal His power and glory to a needy, desperate world. With all the solemnity that we can command we appeal to every member to study God's Word earnestly, to seek first the kingdom of God and His righteousness, and to pray for the outpouring of the Holy Spirit for a finished task (see *Testimonies to Ministers*, pp. 506-512).

THE END: THE UNIQUE VOICE OF ADVENTISTS

Time is short. "Therefore be ye also ready: for in such an hour as ye think not the Son of man cometh" (Matt. 24:44; see also *Testimonies*, vol. 6, p. 406; *Selected Messages*, bk. 1, p. 67).—*Review and Herald*, December 6, 1973.

1974

At the 1973 Annual Council the Holy Spirit overshadowed the assembly, refreshing the hearts of the delegates and producing a deep longing for God. A spirit of revival was felt, and the need for reformation was seen. As a result of this solemn experience, the delegates issued "An Earnest Appeal" to the members of the Seventh-day Adventist Church throughout the world. The appeal acknowledged that the church is in the Laodicean condition (see Rev. 3:14-22), that the character of Christ has not been "perfectly reproduced in His people" (*Christ's Object Lessons*, p. 69), "that the return of Jesus has been long delayed, . . . and that the primary consideration before the Seventh-day Adventist Church is to reorder its priorities individually and corporately so that our Lord's return may be hastened."

The response to this earnest appeal has been impressive in many parts of the world. Ministers have used the appeal as the basis for sermons; and in some areas workers' meetings have been devoted to a study of the issues raised in this appeal. As a result, members everywhere have joined church leaders in the conviction that the Advent Movement's first priority must be spiritual and theological, not organizational. Even if we construct an ideal global enterprise, utilizing the finest of modern business principles, we may fail in our mission if we do not understand clearly how the church is to reach the world with its distinctive message. The church's mission depends on correct theology.

Clear, simple truth will call forth a distinctive Christian experience and life-style. When people understand what God expects them to do they are more apt to cooperate and fulfill His desires.

As delegates to this Annual Council, we believe that the spirit of individual and corporate repentance that resulted in the call by the 1973 Annual Council for revival and reformation must continue to be felt around the world; also that the condition of the church described in the 1973 appeal is still accurate, and that the need for revival, repentance, and reformation remains.

APPENDIX D

But if the church is to advance in spirituality to fulfill its divine mission, Christ and His righteousness must be held up continually before our people, and the entire membership must understand clearly that God is seeking to prepare a people who "keep the commandments of God, and the faith of Jesus" (Rev. 14:12). Such people will have accepted the message to the Laodiceans from the "faithful and true witness." Those who come up to every point, and stand every test, and overcome, be the price what it may, have heeded the counsel of the True Witness, and they will receive the latter rain, and thus be fitted for translation."—*Testimonies*, vol. 1, p. 187.

Such people will have discovered joy and peace in knowing through experience that the Christian's good works are a result of being sustained by divine power, that the "faith of Jesus" produces the character of Jesus.

Such people will have contributed to the vindication of the character of God and the final work of settling the great controversy: "The honor of God, the honor of Christ, is involved in the perfection of the character of His people."—*The Desire of Ages*, p. 671. "The Saviour was deeply anxious for His disciples to understand for what purpose His divinity was united to humanity. He came to the world to display the glory of God, that man might be uplifted by its restoring power. God was manifested in Him that He might be manifested in them. Jesus revealed no qualities, and exercised no powers, that men may not have through faith in Him. His perfect humanity is that which all His followers may possess, if they will be in subjection to God as He was."—*Ibid.*, p. 664. To make this glorious promise a reality in the believer's life "Christ has given His Spirit as a divine power to overcome all hereditary and cultivated tendencies to evil, and to impress His own character upon His church."—*Ibid.*, p. 671. The provision is complete. We are not left alone. "God's ideal for His children is higher than the highest human thought can reach. 'Be ye therefore perfect, even as your Father which is in heaven is perfect.' This command is a promise. The plan of redemption contemplates our complete recovery from the power of Satan. Christ always separates the contrite soul from sin. He came to destroy the works of the devil, and He has made provision that the Holy Spirit shall be imparted to every repentant soul, to keep him from sinning."—*Ibid.*, p. 311.

THE END: THE UNIQUE VOICE OF ADVENTISTS

The manner of life of God's people, seen in their home, neighborhood, and occupational circles, will demonstrate that God is all-wise, loving, and just in the way He governs the universe: "The Lord desires through His people to answer Satan's charges by showing the result of obedience to right principles. . . .
"The purpose which God seeks to accomplish through His people today is the same that He desired to accomplish through Israel when He brought them forth out of Egypt. By beholding the goodness, the mercy, the justice, and the love of God revealed in the church, the world is to have a representation of His character. And when the law of God is thus exemplified in the life, even the world will recognize the superiority of those who love and fear and serve God above every other people on the earth. . . . It is His purpose that those who practice His holy precepts shall be a distinguished people. To the people of God today as well as to ancient Israel belong the words written by Moses through the Spirit of Inspiration: 'Thou art an holy people unto the Lord thy God: the Lord thy God hath chosen thee to be a special people unto himself, above all people that are upon the face of the earth' (Deut. 7:6)."—*Testimonies,* vol. 6, pp. 11, 12.

As church leaders we feel deeply that "the image of Jesus" must be reflected clearly not only in the personal lives of church members but in Adventist sermons, Adventist literature, and Adventist institutions—schools, hospitals, and publishing houses. The answer to the query What is different about the Adventist way? should be obvious to all who come in contact with any aspect of the remnant church. The Adventist goal is primarily quality rather than quantity. Such a goal is reached not by merely doing what other organizations can do equally well, whether such effort be in health care, education, welfare, or even sermons in evangelistic meetings or on Sabbath mornings. Whatever an Adventist does should be distinctively different: "God has ordained that His work shall be presented to the world in distinct, holy lines. He desires His people to show by their lives the advantage of Christianity over worldliness. By His grace every provision has been made for us in all our transaction of business to demonstrate the superiority of heaven's principles over the principles of the world. We are to show that we are working upon a higher plane than that of worldlings."—*Ibid.,* vol. 7, p. 142.

APPENDIX D

The only way by which denominational institutions, or individual professional services in whatever field, can produce such an impact upon the world is first to realize that nothing less than distinctive Christlikeness—apparent and inescapable to all—is their reason for existence, and then to employ only those people who can contribute to this primary reason for establishing Adventist institutions. In the final analysis, it is *people* who are to "reflect the image of Jesus fully" (*Early Writings,* p. 71).

Therefore, we appeal to our members everywhere to consider carefully to what extent they are allowing the Holy Spirit to mold their lives, how committed they are to overcoming all sin by God's grace, how seriously they are looking to Jesus as their example in all things. We are well aware that those represented by the five foolish virgins (see Matthew 25) include Seventh-day Adventists in good and regular standing, even church members who know well the Bible texts to support distinctive Adventist doctrines. These "foolish virgins" are not hypocrites. They know much *about* God but they know very little of Him as a personal Lord who came to "save his people from their sins" (Matt. 1:21).

The wise bridesmaids represent those who allow biblical principles to shape their lives. Whether it be a better health program so that they can be more useful in God's service, more clear-minded in separating truth from error; or a deeper commitment to Sabbath reverence and stewardship of God's material blessings; or a closer examination of those influences that bombard the ear or eye and tend to contaminate the soul, the wise bridesmaids make a daily habit of allowing the Bible and the spirit of prophecy to be the standard for all conduct. The question of Why not? is raised less and less as the wise bridesmaids face life's decisions with a joyful Yes to whatever God asks.

We appeal to all to make serious Bible study, meditation, and prayer an integral part of every day's program. We urge faithful study of the Sabbath school lessons and a systematic reading of the writings of Ellen G. White, especially *The Desire of Ages, Christ's Object Lessons,* and *Steps to Christ.* Jesus spent much of His life studying the Word and praying to His Father for strength, and those who "keep the commandments of God, and the faith of Jesus" can do no less.

Furthermore, Christ-reflecting lives are essential to the gospel

THE END: THE UNIQUE VOICE OF ADVENTISTS

outreach. The more a church member becomes like Christ in character, the more gracious, winsome, and genuinely helpful he will be in his general soul-winning activities, especially in his relationships within his own home and neighborhood. When a generation of Seventh-day Adventists is truly serious about becoming exhibits of what God's grace can do, the moment of final decision by the whole world for or against God will not be long delayed.

The moment of final decision for mankind the world over, often called the close of probation, is long overdue. God has wanted to complete His work on earth at several significant moments since 1844, but many of His people have failed to understand what He waits for; others have been unwilling to cooperate. In 1879 Ellen White wrote: "Because the time is apparently extended, many have become careless and indifferent in regard to their words and actions. They do not realize their danger and do not see and understand the mercy of our God in lengthening their probation, that they may have time to form characters for the future, immortal life. Every moment is of the highest value. Time is granted them, not to be employed in studying their own ease and becoming dwellers on the earth, but to be used in the work of overcoming every defect in their own characters and in helping others, by example and personal effort, to see the beauty of holiness. God has a people upon the earth who in faith and holy hope are tracing down the roll of fast-fulfilling prophecy and are seeking to purify their souls by obeying the truth, and that they may not be found without the wedding garment when Christ shall appear."—*Testimonies,* vol. 4, pp. 306, 307.

We solemnly appeal to our church leaders and members everywhere, to think carefully as to whether they are hindering or hastening the return of Jesus. Our Lord is waiting to intervene in behalf of His church in ways beyond human comprehension, to open doors that will remain closed to human effort—both in the personal lives of dedicated church members and in the breakthrough of public evangelism that will one day startle the world with its clearness and power.

The question Why do we keep Him waiting? should hover over every Adventist home, over every church meeting, large or small. We believe that God is willing to do through this generation what

APPENDIX D

He has wanted to do for many decades. We believe that He ought to be given the opportunity to show through His people today that His grace is sufficient to keep men from falling (see Jude 24), that men and women living amidst temptation and sin can conquer even as Jesus conquered (see Rev. 3:21), and that His way of life produces the happiest, kindest, most trustworthy people on earth.

The urgency of this very late hour, the distress of our world, the fact that many are "looking wistfully toward heaven," and the dwindling days of each person's own probation cry out for a people who will arise to its task and shine. The challenge of God, issued through the prophet Isaiah, is: "Arise, shine; for thy light is come, and the glory of the Lord is risen upon thee. For, behold, the darkness shall cover the earth, and gross darkness the people: but the Lord shall arise upon thee, and his glory shall be seen upon thee. And the Gentiles shall come to thy light, and kings to the brightness of thy rising" (Isa. 60:1-3).

As delegates to this 1974 Annual Council, we believe that the Laodicean message is addressed in a special way to leaders of the church. Therefore, with all the earnestness that we can command, we appeal to all whom God has placed in positions of leadership in the General Conference, in the world divisions, unions, conferences, missions, institutions, and in our churches to lead workers and members into the kind of deep spiritual experience that will enable them "to reflect the image of Jesus fully." This experience will make leadership truly effective in the proclamation of the "everlasting gospel to . . . every nation, and kindred, and tongue, and people" (Rev. 14:6). When the Lord's servants thus bind themselves "to live as Christ himself lived" (1 John 2:6, N.E.B.), the day when the Holy Spirit shall be felt in total latter-rain power will be hastened, the earth will be lightened with the glory of the angel of Revelation 18, and Jesus will come according to His blessed promise.—*Review and Herald,* November 4, 1974.

Indexes

SCRIPTURE

Reference	Page
Genesis 6:5, 9, 11	84
Deuteronomy 28:1, 15	58
1 Samuel 2:30, 31	59
1 Chronicles 12:32	151
2 Chronicles 34:27, 28; 35:21	59
Job 23:10	137
Proverbs 15:1	101
Song of Solomon	157
Isaiah 5:4	61
60:1-3	189
Jeremiah 12:5	152
18:7-10	60
Ezekiel 9:2-4	81, 140
9:4	121
18:31	153
38	40
39	40
Daniel 2	40, 119
7	40, 42, 48, 119
8:25	119
9	39, 41, 43, 46
9:24-27	43, 56
11	119
11:36-39	130
12	119
Jonah 3:10-4:1	59
Micah 7:19	153
Zechariah 9-14	63
Matthew 1:21	95, 187
5:16, 19, 48; 7:21	159
7:21-23	15
7:21-27	92, 116
13:24-30	75
23:37, 38	62
24	42, 53, 113, 119, 120
24:3	98
24:3, 4-7	77, 78
24:14	79, 93, 166, 184
24:30	43
24:34	39
24:37	83, 84, 90
24:37-39	80
24:40, 41	95
24:45, 46	92
24:48-51	97
25	14, 77, 98, 113, 119, 153
25:5	98
25:28	115
25:31-46	116
Mark 4:26-29	65
Luke 15	153
21:25-27	119
John 1:11	62
5:30	122
17:10, 18	103
17:18, 23	135
Acts 3:6	111
Romans 2:28, 29	63
6:7, 12, 14, 17-19	159
8:4	159
9-11	45, 62
10:10	95
11:24	63
12:2	159
13:10	112, 123
16:25, 26	159
1 Corinthians 15:34	159
2 Corinthians 12:9	159
Galatians 3:7-9, 26, 29	47
5:22, 23	96
6:14	122
Ephesians 1:5, 6	136, 146
3:9-11	142
3:10, 16-19	159
4:13 4:13-24	105
4:15, 23, 24	159
5:3-6	155
6:10, 11, 16	159
Philippians 4:19	153
Colossians 1:10, 11, 22, 28	159
3:5-14	155
1 Thessalonians 3:13	42, 159
4:15-17	42
5:2-4	120
5:4-6, 11	118
5:6	65
2 Thessalonians 3:14	124
1 Timothy 6:14	159
2 Timothy 3:1-5	120
Titus 2:13	43
2:13, 14	142
2:14	159
Hebrews 3:19	163
4:16	122, 146
12:14	154
1 Peter 1:15	159
2:12	143
2:24	159
2 Peter 1:9	159
2:5	83
3:3, 4	85
3:11-14	92, 142, 159
3:12	67, 80, 164
1 John 2:3	101
2:6	189
3:2, 3	142
3:3, 7	159
3:24	101
Jude 24	138, 159, 180, 189
Revelation 2:7, 17, 26	159

INDEXES

2:11	156, 159
3:5	159
3:12	156, 159
3:14-22	151, 179, 184
3:20	182
3:21	122, 156, 159, 179, 189
4:19	39
4-22	41, 42
6	120
7:1-3	81
7:1-4	121
12:11	95
12:17	76, 150
13	120
14	97, 99, 120, 136, 150, 182
14:1	123
14:1-5	121
14:6	189
14:6-12	178
14:8-10	181
14:9	125
14:12	16, 74, 84, 90, 92, 95, 112, 136, 142, 143, 146, 159, 179, 185
14:14-16	65, 66
15	129
16	90, 94, 120, 129
16:2	125
17	120
18	126, 182
18:1-4	178, 181
18:1-6	124, 125
19:1, 2, 5	158
19:20	125
20	44

NAMES

Ambrose 169
Andreasen, M. L. v
Augustine 36

Barnabas 168
Barnhouse, Donald 38
Baxter, Richard 172
Bell, L. Nelson 38
Berg, Orly M. 56
Berkhof, L. 36
Berkouwer, G. C. 36
Beyerhaus, Peter 39, 57
Biederwolf, William E. 21
Blodgett, Ralph 56
Boersma, T. 56
Boettner, Loraine 37, 55
Bonar, Horatius 174
Bos, G. 36
Bourdeau, D. T. 76
Braaten, Carl E. 34, 55
Brown, Charlie 108
Brown, William Adams 37
Brunner, Emil 114, 115
Bultmann, Rudolf 33, 34, 54
Bylinsky, Gene 91

Carnell, Edward J. 39
Chafer, L. S. 38
Chaij, Fernando v
Clarke, Adam 36, 55
Clarke, William Newton 37
Clement of Rome 168
Clowney, E. P. 36
Columbus, Christopher 171
Cowper, William 173
Cyprian 168

Damsteegt, P. Gerard 76, 77, 82, 130
Darby, John N. 41
Davis, Thomas A. v
Davis, Wayne H. 31
DeHaan, Martin 31
DeHaan, Richard 38
Dodd, C. H. 32, 54
Douty, Norman 39

Duty, Guy 31
Duveen, Lord Joseph 152
Edwards, Jonathan 36
Elliott, E. B. 172
English, E. Schuyler 38
Erickson, Millard J. 56

Feinberg, Charles L. 38
Foster, Durwood viii
Foxe, John 172

Gaebelein, A. C. 38
Gregory the Great 169
Grounds, Vernon C. 160
Gundry, Robert H. 31, 39

Hartin, Lewis viii
Haskell, Stephen 140
Henry, Carl F. H. 56
Himes, Joshua 174
Hitler, Adolf 29, 79, 175
Hogue, Harland viii

Ignatius 168
Ironsides, Harry A. 38, 51
Irving, Edward 41

Jesus, as Creator 133
 as Example 94, 139
 as High Priest 136
 as Intercessor 102
 as Substitute v, 94

Kahn, Herman 31
Kik, J. Marcellus 37, 55
Kirban, Salem 21
Kissinger, Henry 175
Koch, Kurt E. 82
Kuyper, A. 36

Ladd, George 39, 56
LaHaye, Tim 31
Land, Gary 81
Latimer, Hugh 172
Lindsey, Hal 21, 39, 40, 44, 45, 56
Litch, Josiah 174
Loughborough, J. N. 76

Luther, Martin 171

Mackintosh, C. H. 38
Matteson, J. G. 76
Matthews, Shailer 37
Maxwell, Mervyn 140
McBain, Doward 27
McPherson, David 39, 56
Meadows, Donella H. 31
Melancthon 171
Michelet, Jules 171
Miller, William 174
Moltmann, Jurgen 34, 54
Montgomery, John Warwick 55
Morland, Samuel 170
Moynihan, Daniel P. 26, 27
Mussolini, Benito 175

North, Gary 37

Ockenga, Harold 39
Olson, A. V. 140

Payne, J. Barton 45, 56
Peccei, Aurelio 25
Pierson, Robert H. v
Polycarp 168
Prescott, W. W. 140

Ramm, Bernard 39
Rauschenbusch, Walter 37
Richards, H. M. S., Sr. v
Ridley, Nicholas 172
Robinson, James A. T. 33, 54
Rushdoony, R. J. 37
Rutherford, Samuel 172
Ryrie, Charles C. 38

Schweitzer, Albert 33, 54
Scofield, C. I. 51
Shephard, Norman 37
Silver, Jesse Forrest 170
Smith, Uriah 76
Smith, Wilbur M. 38, 49, 50, 56

191

THE END: THE UNIQUE VOICE OF ADVENTISTS

Solzhenitsyn, Alexander 27, 28
Stalin, Joseph 175
Strong, A. H. 36
Sulpicius Severus 169

Talbot, Louis T. 38
Taylor, Daniel 169
Theobald, Robert 35
Thiessen, Henry 38
Toffler, Alvin 17, 91

Torkelson, Ted v
Torrey, R. A. 38
Vandeman, George E. v
Vanderwaal, C. 56
Waggoner, J. H. 76
Wald, George 31
Walvoord, John 29, 38, 46-48, 56
Ward, C. M. 38
Ward, Hiley H. 20, 91

Warfield, Benjamin B. 36
Wesley, John 172
White, James 37, 55, 76-79, 121
Willoughby, William 30
Wilson, Dwight 53, 57, 82, 175
Wood, Leon J. 28
Woodson, Leslie H. 30
Wycliffe, John 170

SUBJECTS

advent, delay of 98, 101, 123, 141, 145, 161-167
Adventist Review, 13
Andrews University 13
antediluvian world 83-90
apocalypticism 32, 54
apokalupsis 42
Armageddon 26, 29, 31, 40, 52, 120
Atlantic Union College 14

Biola College 56
Buck's Bridge, New York 13

CAT bodyscanners 88
centennials 13
Club of Rome 25
Common Market, The 40, 175
conditional prophecy 45, 53, 58-64
consistent eschatology 33
Cyborgs 88

Dallas Theological Seminary 41, 56
demythology 33, 34
dispensationalism 41, 43, 45, 48, 56
DNA 88
endorphins 88
epiphaneia 42, 43

4-H Club 148
Future Shock 17
Futurism 48, 49

gap theory 46

Harvard University 27
harvest principle 65-82, 96, 105, 121, 148
historicism 49
Holy Spirit 135, 151, 154

inaugurated eschatology 33
Israel, ancient 60-64, 75
   modern state of 28, 39, 41, 43, 46, 48, 49, 60, 62, 64, 141
Jerusalem Conference on Biblical Prophecy 49

labor unions 127, 128
Laodicean Message 151, 179, 180, 184, 185
lasers 88
latter rain 123, 125, 137, 178, 182, 183
law, of God 132-135, 145
Limits to Growth, The 25
loud cry 124-125, 178
love 112-113
mark of the beast 125
Minneapolis General Conference 178

Moody Bible Institute 56
Mutual of New York 22

NATO 175
nonmillennialists 35, 36

October 22, 1844 149

Pace University 26
Pacific School of Religion viii, 55
Parable of Bridegroom 14, 98-105
   Talents 15, 104-111
parousia 42, 43
perfection, moral 106, 111, 144
plagues 120
Plymouth Brethren 38, 41
polymers 88
postmillennialism 35-39, 41
Powerscourt Meeting 41
premillennialism 35-59, 41, 43, 47, 48, 56, 63
preterism 49
pretribulationism 38, 41, 49
probation, close of 72, 73, 76, 156

righteousness 111
righteousness by faith 178, 180
Russia 141
Russo-Japanese Conflict 175

Salk vaccine 88
sanctification 96, 122, 145, 156
sanctuary doctrine 136, 149, 150
Scofield Bible 38, 41
Seabury-Western Theological Seminary 35
sealing work 121-123, 125, 137
seal of God 73
secret rapture 38, 40-46, 52, 55, 56
self-development 105-109, 114
spiritualism 127
Sunday law 97, 128

Talbot Theological Seminary 56
Teflon 88
theology of liberation 34

United Nations 26, 175
University Christian Movement 19

vindication of God 132-138, 145

Western Conservative Baptist Seminary 56

Yosemite National Park 158
Youth's Instructor, The 13

192

We'd love to have you download our catalog of
titles we publish at:

www.TEACHServices.com

or write or email us your thoughts,
reactions, or criticism about this
or any other book we publish at:

TEACH Services, Inc.
254 Donovan Road
Brushton, NY 12916

info@TEACHServices.com

or you may call us at:

518/358-3494

Produced in partnership with
LNFBooks.com

www.ingramcontent.com/pod-product-compliance
Lightning Source LLC
Chambersburg PA
CBHW070537170426
43200CB00011B/2457